LIVING MEMORIES

Belgrave Friends Remembered

edited by
Sandra Moore

Residents of Belgrave Cemetery -
family memories in words and pictures

Friends of Belgrave Cemetery Group

A Friends of Belgrave Cemetery Group publication
© FoBCG 2013

ISBN 978-0-9558972-1-4

9 780955 897214

TABLE OF CONTENTS

Dedicated with awe and gratitude to the memory of the Belgrave generations who went before us to create a better world.

FOREWORD

$\mathbf{B}$elgrave Cemetery opened in 1881 at a time when religion was important, and the love and respect for a lost loved one was shown by the grandeur of their memorial.

In 2004, when some of these fine headstones were vandalised, the Friends of Belgrave Cemetery group was formed. People were united by a common cause; the preservation, conservation and maintenance of this 5½ acre Victorian cemetery.

Their achievements were recognised in the summer of 2013 when Belgrave Cemetery received the prestigious Green Flag Award.

This book 'Living Memories' with its beautiful photographs gives an insight into the lives of some of the people laid to rest in the cemetery. Their strengths and achievements are now immortalised by the memories of their descendants.

We give grateful thanks to Sandra Moore, editor of this book, for her time and effort, and we acknowledge Sandra's meticulous attention to detail in researching and publishing.

'Living Memories - Belgrave Friends Remembered'

Dorothy Marshall
F.o.B.C.G. Chairperson
www.friendsofbelgravecemetery.org.uk

October 2013

INTRODUCTION

When the idea for this book was in its embryonic stage, it was to be an information booklet about Belgrave Cemetery, containing a short history, a more comprehensive discussion about the memorial stones and perhaps more about the wonderful trees that help to keep the air clean and clear of the fumes from the busy Red Hill Way outside the gates. Even the name was chosen, 'Written in Stone'.

Who knows, maybe it will still be written.

However, at this point I volunteered to edit this booklet, and after giving it some thought, I realised that time was not on my side. No, thankfully I wasn't suffering some dreadful ailment, but I realised that, as is usual in the way of things, the relations, friends and close families of the people who are laid to rest at Belgrave Cemetery were getting older. Indeed already many of the graves have no-one left from the original family to tend them.

It came to my mind that what I should be doing, with the help of the Friends of Belgrave Cemetery, was searching for memories, about the people laid to rest, before those memories were forgotten and lost forever. But not necessarily the well-known, well-off people about whom much has already been written. Not the landowners or mayors of the city, of whom there are several resting here, but the working people, the folk who helped build the strong economic structure that made 20th century Leicester one of the richest cities in the world. Men and women who stood for long hours working at machines, who brought up large families and sent their husbands and sons off to war to make even greater sacrifices, with little or no praise or acknowledgement. I was sure their stories were well worth telling.

So began a journey through the life of the old village of Belgrave and beyond.

It soon became clear that many of the late Victorians and early Edwardians laid to rest in the newly opened cemetery in 1881, were not necessarily Belgrave born and bred. Rather, they or their parents had moved to Leicester during the mid 1800s seeking better working conditions with more pay and enhanced opportunities. Many of the men had left brutal employment on the land; and the girls, little more than children, along with young single women had realised that domestic service gave them no freedom to 'better themselves'. The chance to move at will from hosiery industry to boot and shoe, to elastic web making or shop work must have been very tempting.

Belgrave, at this time was still a select little village based around The Green in Bath Street, Belgrave Hall near the church, and down the Loughborough Road, where the large imposing architectural houses standing in their own grounds were the homes of the well-to-do and the factory owners.

To get to Leicester from Belgrave was to journey through fields rapidly being filled with new housing and across a stream, the Willow Brook, (now under the road near Sainsbury's on the Belgrave Road) where the road branched off towards Barkby. Hard to imagine now.

Soon new red brick terraced streets appeared, with factories wedged in amongst the houses. These provided not only homes for the new influx of labour but also a nearby source of employment. This gave the owners a steady and continuous supply of labour, and I suppose 'kept the workers in their place'. Also many beer houses, off-licensed premises and working men's clubs would appear, dotted amongst the streets. Even new churches appeared, St Michael and All Angels Church, Claremont Street and Harrison Road Methodist Chapels for example. Every need catered for!

"The Friends of Belgrave Cemetery need your help". Our initial advertisement in the Leicester Mercury, a plea for help from their readers, people of Leicester and previous residents of Belgrave produced an excellent response. Information in many forms, from brief notes, to whole family books already written, census forms and notes on envelopes came in thick and fast and it has continued to do so on and off for the last couple of years.

From the information we received it soon became very apparent what hard lives the majority of our ancestors lived.

Some families were haunted by contagious disease, losing not only very young babies but adult children and grandchildren in rapid succession. There were several suicides, sons lost in both the Great War and the Second World War and husbands who deserted young wives and families. But what has stayed with me is the number of babies stillborn, and the large number of infants who died before reaching 5 years old. Living in 2013, we are truly blessed.

But what also comes over in the hard lives of these, our ancestors, is that they had little help from the state and tried so desperately not to resort to charity. The workhouse was the very last resort and I think some ended their lives there only because they were carried in by others. They would never have walked unaided into these dreaded places.

Many of the aged survivors of these large families, who had lost child after child, were reported as "still being a jolly person", always laughing, always with a smile on their faces and wanting to help others. Perhaps we living today should take some lessons.

Not only information came to us but wonderful photographs; portraits, snapshots from holidays, soldiers in uniform, couples with their horses, men and women at their employment. Some are shown in their best clothes at the photographer's studio and some in clothes obviously provided by the photographer; some on their allotments, or at their hobbies; some in their new motor cars; some bashful in front of the camera and others smiling broadly.

Belgrave as a village is a fading memory now. The area has new people working just as hard as our parents and grand-parents did, and they are probably totally unaware of their heritage provided by our ancestors.

I hope that the Friends of Belgrave Cemetery have achieved what we set out to do and that readers of this book and visitors to Belgrave Cemetery will catch a flavour of the times past and feel the heritage that is ours.

The intention of 'Living Memories' was to record the lives of the ordinary people resting here. But we discovered that there are no ordinary people resting here - every one of them was unique in their own way.

Now as I walk around the cemetery I recognise names and there, suddenly, I see their photograph, they are smiling into the camera. The stone melts away and the person laid to rest has a face again and is not just a name written on a stone.

Truly our cemetery has come alive!

Sandra Moore
October 2013

ACKNOWLEDGMENTS

Many people must be thanked for their contribution to this book.
First and foremost all the splendid people who kindly put a halt on their busy lives to search out papers, photographs, birth and death certificates, grave deeds, census forms, made contact with relatives and generally racked their brains for details:

Roger Beall

Carole Campbell

Corinne Chippendale

Martyn & John Collier

Pat Cox

Jean Crofts

Kathleen Dixey

Mark Gamble

Elaine Graeme

Glyn John Hatfield

Val Holliland

Robert Horner

Garth Hoskins

Pauline Hulbert née Hunt

Pat Keeling

Mollie Knight

Carol Lincoln

Mrs Dorothy Marshall

Roy Mason

Lesley Moore

Sandra Moore

Mr Keith R. Powell

Trevor Radford

Robert Savage

Mr & Mrs Shaw

Marlene Robinson

Sandra Smith

Mrs Sue Stanley

Beverley Taylor née Squires

Jan Tebbatt née Heggs

Mrs Anita Tebbutt

Mavis B. Timson

J.E. Tomlinson

Mr Paul Tuff

Mrs Odette Wells

Mrs C.M. Welsh

Marilyn Whatley

Colin Wilkinson

Mr G.L.Wolfe & Mrs B. Knight

Susan Wyatt

Also to all the members of the Friends of Belgrave Cemetery Group committee who have given unstinting and sometimes bemused support to me, in particular Joy May our Record officer for double checking grave plot numbers and details; Chairwoman Dorothy Marshall and Deputy Chair John Dixey, who not knowing me very well, trusted me with the production of this 'booklet', giving only a sharp intake of breath as more and more entries turned it into a book and production costs grew as each week passed. Thank you for your support and confidence. I hope I didn't let you down! To Dr John Sutton for help with soldiers details.

But lastly and most importantly, my partner, Nick Fathers, who has supported, advised, listened to tales of woe, explosions of disbelief, fed and watered me and has provided technical support without which I could not have completed the project. Only we two know how much I am indebted to him. I shall be very tired if he calls in the favour!

Thank you all for your forbearance at the length of time this has taken. I hope you all think it was worth the journey, as I do.

HOW TO USE THIS BOOK

The entries in this book are arranged first of all in Cemetery Section order, that is, Sections A, B, C, D and E. (See the plan of Belgrave Cemetery for the location of each Section).

Within each Section the entries are in Plot Number order, and then in alphabetical order of Surname.

The end of each Plot Number is indicated by a small open book symbol 📖.

At the end of the book is an index, listing all the entries in alphabetical Surname order, indicating on which page and in which Section and Plot Number, they can be found. For example;

Godsall, Gladys Beatrice (1904 - 1993)   D1079   97

Gladys Godsall is buried in Cemetery Section D, Plot 1079 and her story can be found on Page 97.

A second index lists all the entries in Section and Plot Number order and indicates on which page they can be found. For example;

D1079	**Godsall**, Gladys Beatrice (1904 - 1993)	97
D1079	**Godsall**, May Louisa (1878 - 1939)	98
D1079	**Godsall**, William (1877 - 1955)	99

Gladys Beatrice, May Louisa and William are all buried in Cemetery Section D, Plot 1079 and their stories can be found on the pages indicated.

PLAN OF BELGRAVE CEMETERY

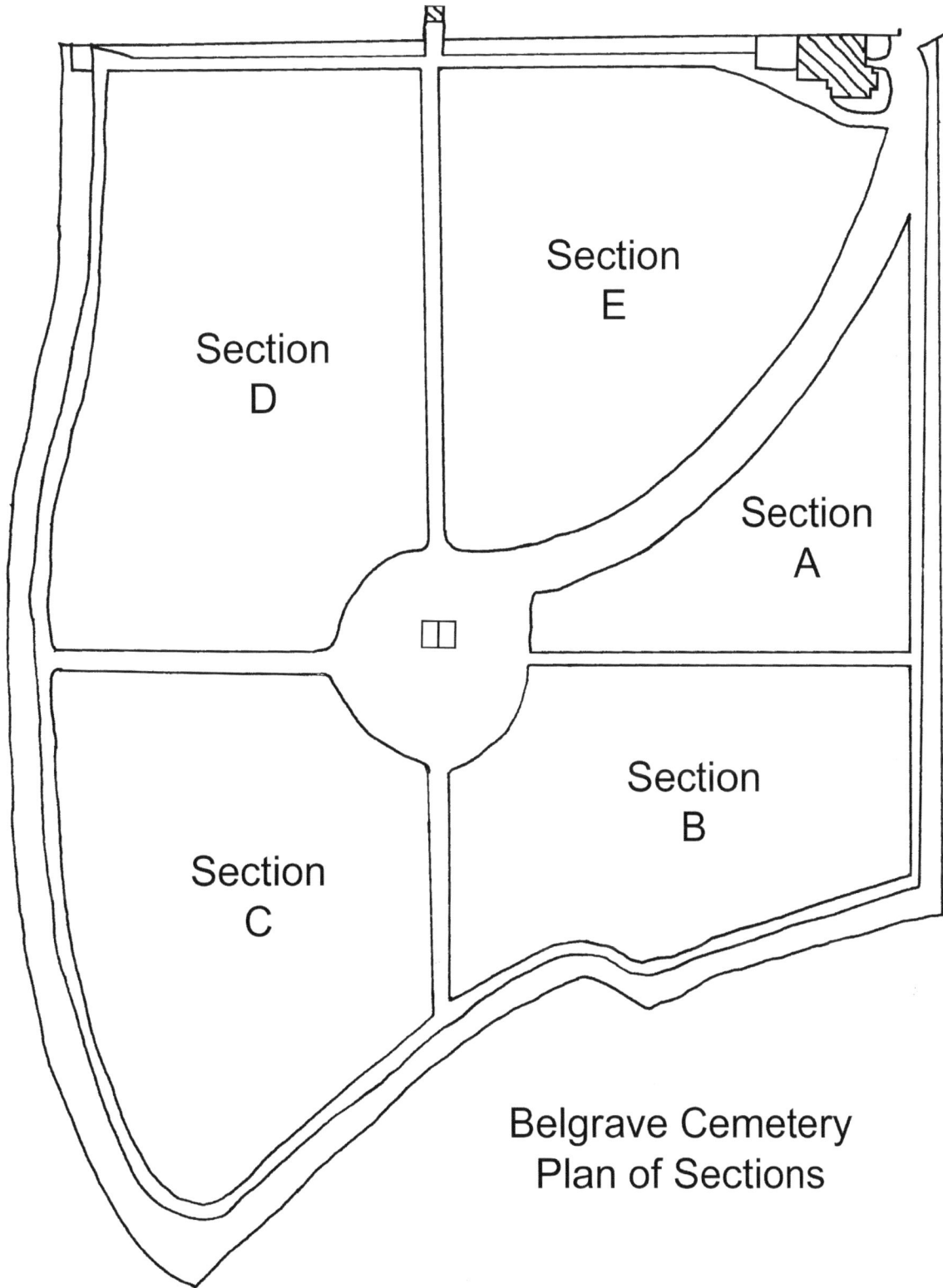

Section E

Section D

Section A

Section B

Section C

Belgrave Cemetery
Plan of Sections

Collier, George Harry (1863 - 1948)

George Harry was born on 21st November 1863 in Groby, Leicestershire to William and Ann Collier. *(See Plot A223)* Up to the age of approximately ten years he lived with his parents at the Rookery in Groby, but then they moved to Leire Street, in Belgrave.

We know little about his earlier life, but we do know that he had become a Cashier by 1891.

On 4th June 1892 he married Mary Jane Wilkes and they had three children.

Meanwhile, in his business career, he became the first Collier family member to be involved with the shoe trade, followed by the next two generations who were Directors or proprietors of local shoe companies.

George was to become Managing Director of Smith, Faire and Co. Ltd, boot manufacturers by the time he retired.

George became a well known figure in the local cricket scene. He took up membership of his adoptive local team Belgrave Town, being Captain during three memorable years, 1903-1905 when they were Champions of the 1st Division Leicester City League.

George has many descendants who are keen on cricket, culminating in his Great Grandson, David Gordon Collier, who on 13th December 2008 was appointed Chief Executive Officer of the England and Wales Cricket Board.

George was also associated with the work of St Michael and All Angels Church, Belgrave.

He died on 8th March 1948 at 46 Holmfield Road, Leicester, aged 84.

Collier, Mary Jane (1871 - 1956)

Mary Jane Wilkes was born on 18th April 1871 in Belgrave, Leicester.

She married George Harry Collier on 4th June 1892 in Belgrave and they had three children, Gladys May born 1894, Cyril Harry born 1900 and Gwendolen Mary born 1911, (one of whom is still alive at a lively 102!)

Mary Jane died on 30th July 1956, aged 85 and was laid to rest with George Harry who died on 8th March 1948 at 46 Holmfield Road, Leicester, aged 84.

📖

l to r: Mrs H.H. Collier (Auntie Ginnie), Mrs A. Vann (Auntie Annie), Mrs G.H. Collier, unknown, Mr H.H. Collier, Mr G.H. Collier. Photograph believed to have been taken in the back garden of 'Craigmore', Holmfield Road, Leicester

Kirk, Leonard Hairsine (1888 - 1921)

Leonard was born at Wallingfen, Yorkshire on 19th July 1888, second son of William, a butcher, and Henrietta Kirk née Underwood.

He married Florence Agnes Law daughter of Alfred Paul Law and Hannah Law née Measures in the latter quarter of 1915.

Florence was born in 1886 in Belgrave, Leicester, one of five children, namely Joseph, Alexander, Elizabeth and William with Florence being the youngest.

By the 1901 Census, Florence is described as a Pupil school teacher, and in the 1911 Census at her parent's house she is classed as a School Teacher, working for Leicestershire County Council. It is likely that this is where she met Leonard as in the 1911 Census, Leonard is living as a boarder to Mrs Sarah Cooper in Asfordby and his occupation is a school teacher, employed by the Education Committee. Interestingly a Florence Law, single, aged 24 years, is also listed as boarding at Mrs Cooper's and her occupation is listed as a school teacher employed by the Education Committee. It would seem that they met through their employment and by boarding at the same place but strange that Florence is recorded both as being at home with her parents at 27 Canon Street and simultaneously in Asfordby.

Leonard's occupation at the time of his death in 1921 is recorded as Elementary Schoolmaster (assistant). By this time Leonard and Florence were living at 27 Canon Street, Belgrave, presumably with Florence's parents Alfred & Hannah Law.

Leonard fought in the Great War, initially in the Army Service Corps (Regimental No. 307375), later in the Kings Royal Rifles Corps (Regimental No. 202835) and finally as a Sapper in the Meteorological Section of the Royal Engineers (Regimental No. 361711). According to army sources, the last position is likely to have been a less onerous posting presumably due to being wounded.

On 12th May 1921, at home at 27 Canon Street, Belgrave, he died of "Sub acute Malignant Endocarditis, 4 months, no pain." This is possibly due to being wounded as he is listed in the Army War Graves Commission website. His eldest brother, Dennis W Kirk was present at his death and was also executor of his will.

Leonard is laid to rest with Florence, who died 3rd May 1957 aged 71. She was living at 47 Jermyn Street, Belgrave at the time of her death. Both Leonard's father-in-law, Alfred Paul Law, who died 9th August 1926 aged 73 and his mother-in-law, Hannah Law, who died on 30th November 1925 aged 73 years were still living at 27 Canon Street up to their deaths.

📖

Wilkinson, Clara (1870 - 1961)

Clara was born in 1870 to Henry and Sarah Ann Wilkinson. She remained single and was part of the property management team of the family. She was still involved with some property in the Britannia Street area in the 1940s. Our contributor's sister remembers her going every week on the tram from where she lived on Loughborough Road, Belgrave with a leather purse strapped around her waist to collect rent. She lived into her 90's and our contributor lived near her and knew her well.

Clara died in March 1961, her address being given as 24 Argyle Street.

Wilkinson (snr), Henry (1849 - 1902)

Henry Wilkinson was born on 15th June 1849. His father, Samuel was a gardener and green grocer and had a shop at 11 Northgate Street, Leicester.

Henry married Sarah Ann Cockrayne (born 5th June 1850) on 30th August 1868 at the parish church of St. Margaret's, Leicester. On their marriage certificate it is stated that he is a weaver, with no occupation shown for Sarah Ann, and they are both resident in Britannia Street, Leicester.

They had five sons Joseph (1873), Henry, known as Harry (1875), Arthur Albert (1877), Edwin (1880), and Alfred (1886) and a daughter Clara (1870) who never married.

Henry became the proprietor of the Victoria Model Lodging House at 55 Britannia Street, Leicester, which was designed and built for Henry by Alfred Hinds in 1887. The building, which can still be seen just off the Belgrave Road, is renowned for the decorative terracotta panels on the outside wall, depicting an Englishman, Irishman, Scot and Welshman *(see next page)* and has been the subject of many articles in the local newspaper over the years.

The family also owned other property in the Britannia Street area which was housing for women with families and single people. They were managed by Henry (Harry), Joseph, Alfred and Clara Wilkinson.

Henry Wilkinson snr died on 17th December 1902, aged 54 years. His occupation was given as Lodging House Keeper, 55 Britannia Street, Leicester.

Decorative terracotta tiles on wall of 55 Britannia Street, Leicester,
depicting Scotsman and Irishman *(above)* and Welshman and Englishman *(below)*

Wilkinson, (jnr) Henry (1875 - 1953)

Harry Wilkinson was born in 1875 and was known as Harry, son of Henry Wilkinson, lodging house keeper and his wife Sarah Ann Wilkinson.

He managed, along with his brothers Joseph, Alfred and sister Clara, the property which his father owned as well as the Victoria Model Lodging House in Britannia Street, Leicester.

He played rugby for many years with the Leicester Football Club (Tigers) starting in the 1890s and it is believed he played until around 1910. He was also a good amateur boxer, as was his brother Joseph who fought many times at the National Sporting Club. He opened and ran a lodging house in Mill Lane, Melton Mowbray. This was pulled down when the road was widened.

Harry's other brother Alfred was a very good Amateur Athletics Association runner and won many trophies, medals and prizes as a sprinter around the country. He became a shopkeeper in later years.

Brother Arthur Albert was a pawnbroker and publican, and Edwin was a Shoe Riveter, marrying twice, for the second time in 1906.

Funeral of Henry Wilkinson snr (1902) left to right Clara, Alfred, Edwin, Joseph,
Arthur Albert, Henry jnr (Harry), Sarah Ann Wilkinson.
Note the glass domes over the floral tributes

All the brothers were very much into sport and a quote taken from the Leicester Mercury called them a "well known sporting family"

Harry died in May 1953 aged 77 years and rests with his father Henry died aged 54 in 1902, mother Sarah Ann died 1921 aged 71 and sister Clara died 1961 aged 90.

Baker, Emma (1882 - 1915)

Emma Pretty was born in 1882 second daughter to Emma Pretty née Bramley and Alfred Pretty who had married in 1877. They were to have a family of eight altogether.

In the 1891 Census she is living at 10 Lead Street with her parents and siblings and in the 1901 Census they are at 33 Taylor Street.

Little is known about her earlier life but she was at one point employed as a feeder in the Printing trade.

In 1903 she married Albert E. Baker, a carpenter who had been born in 1880 and they had three children. Evelyn Emma Baker born 1903, Cyril Baker born 1906 and Dorothy Baker born 1909.

In 1905 to 1908 the family were living at 20 Unity Avenue, and at that time took in Ada her orphaned sister when she left school at fourteen.

Emma died very young aged 33 years on 6th January 1915 whilst the family were living at 178 Harrison Road, Belgrave, Leicester

Mawby, Elizabeth Annie (1848 - 1920)

Elizabeth Annie Bramley was born in 1848, to Caroline and Edward Bramley. She had two sisters, Harriet born 1851 and Emma, born 1858. All through her life she was known as Annie.

On 12th January 1866 she married Samuel Henry Roper, in Chesterfield, Derbyshire. They were both of them aged 18.

There were two children from this marriage, Samuel Henry Roper born in 1872 and Bertie Roper born 1874.

Unfortunately Annie's husband Samuel died at the young age of approximately 42 years on 13th April 1890. *(See Plot A160)*

1891 found Elizabeth Annie both a widow and a licensed victualler at 239 Belgrave Gate, known as The Durham Ox.

Elizabeth remarried in 1891, this time to Nathaniel Mawby but there were no children of the marriage. By 1901 she was keeping a hotel at 290-292 Belgrave Gate.

In 1920 she had become a publican at The Wheatsheaf Inn, Burton-on-Trent, Staffordshire, where she was to die, but by the date of her death, her son Samuel Henry Roper was the publican, calling himself Samuel Henry Roper-Bramley.

Elizabeth Annie died on 5th April 1920 aged 68 years.

Pretty, Emma (1858 - 1904)

Emma Bramley was born in 1858 in Chester, to Caroline Bramley 1822 - 1887 and Edward Bramley. She was the youngest of three girls, Elizabeth Annie, born in 1848, and Harriet born in 1851.

She was employed as a glove hand and eventually married Alfred Pretty born in 1857, in 1877. They were to have eight children, the first, Alf, was born in 1877 and lived for only three months.

Next came Annie, 1879, Emma 1882, Julia 1885, Harriett 1886, Caroline (who was born blind) 1889, Ada 1891 and finally Maud 1896.

Alfred died aged 39 years in 1896 in Leicester Workhouse before his last child, Maud, was born.

Ada was to marry and become the mother of Ivy Hales (eventually Beechey) *(See Plot C383)*

Emma Pretty died in 1904 aged 46 years and was laid to rest at Belgrave Cemetery to be joined later by her daughter Emma Baker, aged 33 years on 6th January 1915, and Emma Pretty's sister Elizabeth Annie Mawby who died on 5th April 1920 aged 68 years. (It was Elizabeth Mawby who purchased the grave)

Emma Baker's husband Albert was to die in 1941. *(See other family members in Plots C383 & A160)*

Roper, Samuel Henry (1848? - 1890)

There is very little information about Samuel, what is known is that his birth date varies between 1844 and 1852!

The 1851 Census puts him as seven years old, living in Humberstone Gate with a widowed mother and siblings.

On 12th January 1866 he married Elizabeth Annie Bramley, in Chesterfield, Derbyshire and his date of birth is recorded as 1844, when they were both 18 years old!

There were two children from this marriage, Samuel Henry Roper who was born in 1872 and Bertie Roper born in 1874.

In the 1881 Census, when a Commercial traveller, boarding at Stamford with Annie, he gave his age as 35 years. Even the cemetery records differ from the age on the headstone!

Samuel Henry snr had a comparatively short life, however, dying around the age of 42 years, approximately!

It was Samuel that bought this grave plot, and when he died in April 1890, he was laid to rest with his mother-in-law, Caroline Bramley, who died on 27th November 1887, aged 65 years, and his sister-in-law Harriet Sheppard née Bramley who died on 19th February 1889 aged 38 years. *(See also family plots A159 & C383)*

Manship, Arthur (1883 - 1919)

Arthur Manship was born on the 6th December 1883 in the parish of St. Mark, Leicester. He was the son of Leicester freeman William Manship (1851-1939) and his wife Harriet, née Sanders (1851-1894).

On the 17th August 1900, at HMS President, London, he enlisted for the Royal Navy, aged 16 years 8 months. Despite being judged of very good character, his service with the navy ended on the 1st July 1902, when it was recorded that he had run away from HMS Pembroke, the Navy's barracks at Chatham.

In the meantime, on the 7th June 1902 Arthur Manship, under the assumed name of Arthur Neaves, had attested to the army and had been appointed to the 14th Hussars.

The 14th Hussars had been sent to South Africa soon after the outbreak of the Second Boer War, which had begun in 1899. Arthur Neaves (Regimental No. 4928) joined the regiment in South Africa in the aftermath of the war, serving there from 9th October 1902 to 3rd May 1903.

On his return to England he was taken up by the navy as a deserter and imprisoned from 4th July to the 12th August 1903. He then returned to the army.

During December 1904 Arthur Neaves was transferred to the 13th Hussars and embarked aboard ship for service in India. The 13th Hussars had been serving in India from September 1904. They were occupied in the same activities that took up the time of all soldiers who guarded the jewel of empire - military training exercises, visits to hill stations away from the heat, sporting events, arms and shooting exercises, and ceremonial parades were the norm. However, Arthur Neaves was to take part in the greatest ceremonial event ever seen in India – The Great Durbar of 1911.

The 13th Hussars had moved to Meerut in October 1910 and it was from there that they moved to Delhi to take part in the Durbar in December 1911. The Durbar was made up of more than 50,000 British and Indian troops formed up for a massive ceremonial parade before their King and Emperor George V and Queen Mary, in commemoration of the coronation.

The 13th Hussars furnished escort to the king when he presented new colours to seven British and three Indian regiments on the 11th December 1911. After the Durbar the regiment also escorted Queen Mary on a visit to Agra. Arthur Neaves received the Coronation Durbar medal that was issued to mark the occasion. On the 1st January 1912 Arthur Neaves (Regimental No. 6914) was promoted to Corporal.

In June 1914 and at the end of his period of engagement Arthur began his return journey to England. He arrived in a Europe that was in turmoil. With the outbreak of the Great War he was recalled to the army and was engaged with the 3rd Reserve Cavalry Division.

In 1918 the Great War ended with the Armistice and soon thereafter, on the 19th November 1918, at Leicester Registry Office, Arthur was married to Minnie Haywood under his assumed name Arthur Neaves.

Minnie was the sister of Tom Haywood, who was married to Arthur's niece Edith Weston, the eldest daughter of Susannah Weston, née Manship.

Sometime after his marriage Arthur was promoted to Sergeant as is shown in the photograph. Unfortunately, on the 12th March 1919, suffering the effects of pneumonia, Arthur Neaves died at Winchester. The officer at Easton Military Hospital, Winchester, recorded his death in the name of Sergeant Arthur Neaves, 13th Hussars.

The following day an announcement was made in the Leicester Daily Mercury newspaper:

Saturday, March 15, 1919. Page 10.

'DEATHS

MANSHIP

On March 12th, at Winchester Military Hospital, of pneumonia,

Arthur second son of Mr. and Mrs. W. Manship, 9, Gas-street, age 35.'

According to Phyllis, daughter of Arthur's sister, Susannah, the body of Arthur Manship was returned to Leicester by railway train. She also recalls that the Union flag which draped Arthur's coffin was given to her mother after his burial at Belgrave Cemetery, Leicester.

Arthur Manship is interred with his mother, Harriet, who died 29th March 1894 aged 42 years and his father, William Manship, who died 20th June 1939 aged 83 years. His wife Minnie Neaves died at Cromer, Norfolk, on the 18th October 1975, aged 79 years. The couple left no children.

Collier, Ann (1840 - 1900)

Ann Mason was born in 1840 at Ratby to John and Fanny Mason. Her father John was a bricklayer.

We know little of her early life until her banns are read out three times at Ratby Church. She was to marry William Collier, aged 24, a joiner. Ann was 20 years old when the marriage took place on 19th December 1860.

In 1861, we find she is sharing a house in Groby with not only new husband William, but William's brother Richard, who is a lodger.

Ten years later the couple are living at the Rookery, Groby and Ann has given birth to George Harry, now aged seven and daughter Sarah Ann aged nine.

According to the Groby parish records, another son, Arthur, was baptised on 4th November 1873 but died within the year.

By the 1881 Census, the family seem to have moved between 1872 and 1879 from Groby to 43 Leire Street, Belgrave. Ann has given birth to William Mason Collier in 1872 at Groby but Herbert Horace and Charles Collier were born in Belgrave in 1879 and 1880 respectively.

The 1891 Census shows William and Ann have moved further up Leire Street to number 88. Daughter Sarah is now a dressmaker, son George Harry is a cashier and William Mason Collier, a cotton spinner whilst Herbert Horace is still at school.

On 28th June 1900 Ann Collier died at her home in Belgrave, aged 60 years. She was buried in Belgrave cemetery with her two sons, William Mason who died 1890 aged 22, and Charlie, died 1890 aged 10 years. She was joined by husband William who died on 18th January 1910, aged 73 years.

Collier, William (1836 - 1910)

William was born to Joseph and Sarah Collier in 1836, his baptism taking place on 9th July 1836 according to the Ratby Parish Registers. His father Joseph was a labourer and both he and Sarah lived in Groby.

Between his birth and marriage we have little information about him but he came from a long line of wheelwrights in Groby and so there were plenty of family members to teach him about woodworking and he spent all of his life as a carpenter and joiner as we shall see.

We next hear of William when the banns for his marriage were read in Ratby Church on 25th November, 2nd and 9th December 1860. On 19th December 1860 he married Ann Mason. He was 24. He was a joiner and Ann's father a bricklayer. Next year, in the 1861 Census William was now classed as a Carpenter and Joiner.

In 1871 the couple were living at the Rookery, Groby and William still employed as a Carpenter. Their second son Charlie was born in 1880.

By the 1881 Census, the family had moved from Groby to 43 Leire Street, Belgrave, this is evident by the place date details of the children on the census. Between 1872 and 1879, William Mason Collier was born in 1872 at Groby but Herbert Horace and Charles Collier were born in Belgrave in 1879 and 1880 respectively.

Unfortunately they were to lose William Mason Collier on 20th May 1890, aged 22 followed by Charlie Collier on 22nd December 1890 aged 10 years.

The 1891 Census shows William and Ann have moved further up Leire Street to number 88. Sarah is now a dressmaker, son George Harry is a cashier and William Mason Collier, a cotton spinner whilst Herbert Horace is still at school.

On 28th June 1900 Ann Collier died at her home in Belgrave, aged 60 years.

In the 1901 Census, William, daughter Sarah Ann and son Herbert Horace are still together in their home, Herbert Horace has become a draper's traveller. (He was to eventually have a draper's shop in Liverpool with his cousin, one of Richard's sons, Frank.) Whilst searching the census, it was noted by our contributor that at number 84 Leire Street is Harry Vann. He was to marry Sarah Ann Collier later.

William died on 18th January 1910 aged 73 years, at 260 Harrison Road, just round the corner from Leire Street. He was still registered as a carpenter and joiner at his death. He was buried with his wife Ann, and their young sons William Mason and Charlie.

📖

Billington, Edward (1886 - 1917)

Born in 1886, and known as Ted, Edward was the youngest son of Thomas and Eliza Billington, Thomas being the licensee of what was then known as the Bull's Head Beer House in Bath Street, Belgrave. Unfortunately not a great deal is known about Edward.

There is however, a newspaper report dated 1894 telling of an accident with a horse and carriage driven by a Mr J. Cave, whose family had set off on a picnic to Woodhouse Eaves.

For no apparent reason the horse bolted near the 'Champion' public house on the Checketts Road and Loughborough Road corner and Mr Cave managed to get the horse to turn smartly off the main thoroughfare and away from the dangers there and into Bath Street, unfortunately colliding with a group of children who were looking in a sweet shop window.

Edward, aged eight at the time, had his thigh broken and was taken to the Royal Infirmary along with two young sisters from another family who appeared to have similar injuries.

The horse broke the window of the shop and sent glass flying into the establishment. Fortunately the daughter of the owner had just gone from the shop to have her dinner and so was unharmed. There must have been a great deal of noise that day in Belgrave!

In 1901, aged 15 years, Edward was still living at home and his occupation was listed in the census as a 'Butcher's Apprentice'.

At some point he went to fight in France during the Great War where he was killed in action on 28th June 1917 aged 32 years

We have only one photograph of him, a good looking, smartly dressed young man.

Edward is buried in France but is remembered both on the war memorial at Arras in France and on the memorial stone of his mother and father, Thomas and Eliza Billington in Belgrave Cemetery. He is also mentioned on the war memorial in St Peter's Church, Belgrave, (now closed) his local parish church.

Billington, Eliza (1848 - 1915)

Born in 1848 to Francis and Ann Greenwood, little is known at present about Eliza Greenwood. She married Thomas Billington on 3rd March 1867 and both the bride and groom along with their witnesses (one of whom was a Richard Hallam, a relation of the soon to be Alderman perhaps?) made their mark of a cross on the certificate, so we must presume that none of the party could read or write. (Sometimes friends who could read and write would not embarrass others who couldn't by just signing with their mark)

It would appear Eliza, like so many women at that time, brought up a sizeable family of 7, whilst also helping her husband at the turn of the century in his business at the Bull's Head Beer House at 4-6 Bath Street, a building still on the corner of Loughborough Road. Older family members remembered that the pub, which it became, was always kept spotless with shiny brass fittings and well scrubbed floors.

Eliza died, aged 67 years on 10th May 1915, at home in Victoria Road North, Belgrave, where it is presumed that the couple moved when their son Oliver took over the business.

We have to be grateful that she didn't live to feel the loss of her youngest son Edward, when he was killed in Arras in 1917.

Billington, Thomas (1846 - 1926)

Thomas Billington was born 5th September 1846 in Belgrave, eldest son of William, a Framework Knitter, and Sarah Billington.

He married Eliza Greenwood on 3rd March 1867 when according to their marriage certificate, he too was a framework knitter and both he and Eliza were resident at 51 Checketts Road, living with Eliza's father.

By 1891 Thomas, Eliza and family were living at and running the Bull's Head beer house, at 4 - 6 Bath Street, Belgrave.

There were at least seven children, four boys and three girls, Sarah Ann, born 1869, Oliver, 1875, Walter, 1879, John William, 1881, Ada, 1883, Edward, 1885, Ethel, 1887.

Family rumour has it that Thomas and Eliza also had property in Belgrave. It was known that Eliza had 'the business head' but unfortunately died first. It would seem that Oliver, Thomas's son, took over the running of the Bull's Head sometime in between the 1901 and 1911 Census.

No paperwork or photos survive of Thomas or Eliza, except details from various census records. After his retirement as a licensed victualler and the death of Eliza, Thomas went to live at 15 Linford Street, Belgrave.

Thomas died at the Castle Inn, Caldecote in the County of Rutland, on 12th February 1926, aged 79 years. What he was doing that far from his home in Belgrave, no-one knows.

He is laid to rest with Eliza, who died on 10th May 1915, aged 67 years in Belgrave Cemetery and Edward Billington his son, killed in action 1917 is remembered on the memorial stone. According to the cemetery records however, also in the grave is little Ethel Voss, aged one, who died in the Fever Hospital in March 1910, another family member, not named on the stone

Vann, Harry William (1864 - 1915)

Harry William Vann was born in Port Louis, Mauritius sometime in 1864. There are few details about his earlier life or when he came to England but he was certainly living in Leire Street with his aunt, Ann Irons, just a few doors away from the Collier family during the 1901 Census.

He married Sarah Ann Collier on 25th July 1903 at St. Michael and All Angels Church, Belgrave and she became known as Annie Vann.

They were married for almost twelve years before Harry died on 22nd July 1915, aged 51 years.

Vann, Sarah Ann (1862 - 1950)

Sarah Ann Collier was born in 1862 at Groby and was always known as Annie. Her father, William, was a carpenter and joiner.

She had five siblings, George Harry, (1864) William Mason, (1872) who died at 22 years, Arthur, (1873) who died within the same year, Horace Herbert (1879). Charlie, (1880) who was to die aged 10 years.

By 1881, the family were living at 43 Leire Street and by the next census they had moved further up the street to number 88. Sarah Ann was now a dressmaker, and the family can remember Auntie Annie after her marriage, being a tailoress and remodelling Cyril Collier's cricket blazer when the styles changed.

By the time the 1901 Census was completed, Sarah's mother Ann had died of bronchitis in 1900 and Sarah was now running the home of her father William and her brother Horace Herbert, a draper's traveller.

However on the same census sheet, Harry Vann was living with his aunt a couple of doors away and soon he and Sarah were married on 25th July 1903 and she was now known as Annie Vann. They went to live at 66 Jermyn Street, Belgrave.

Sadly Harry died just a few days away from their twelfth wedding anniversary, on 22nd July 1915 aged 50 years. He was buried at Belgrave Cemetery. Sarah was to continue on until 18th December 1950 when she died aged 89 years. Harry and Sarah are buried next to Sarah's parents, William and Ann Collier, and their two young sons, Charlie and William Mason. *(See Plot A223)*

Calvert, Eliza (1873 - 1950)

Eliza Woodier was the daughter of John & Julia Woodier. She was born in Coventry, Warwickshire and the family moved to Leicester in the 1870s.

From 1891 until 1911, censuses show she was a Boot and Shoe Machinist.

Eliza married Walter J. Calvert in April 1914 at the age of 41.

Little else is known about Eliza.

She died in June 1950 aged 78 and was buried on 28th June 1950. She was living at 32 Hazelwood Road, Leicester at the time of her death.

Thompson, John Ernest (1887 - 1891)

Just after mid-day on Saturday 26th September 1891, four year old John said goodbye to his Mum, Amy, as he went off to play. That would be the last time Amy would see him alive.

John was the eldest child of John Henry Thompson and Amy Thompson (née Woodier).

Two of Amy's younger brother's (John Ernest's uncles), Henry, aged seven and Lewis 'Albert' Woodier, aged four, called on John at his home, 37 Rodney Street, Leicester and off they went to play, taking with them some packed lunch.

Before leaving the house Amy told them not to go near the canal at Abbey Park.

Later that afternoon the 'Drags' were called and John's body was recovered from the canal. By the time he was taken to Dr Lewitt's surgery, Dr Lewitt considered he had died approximately 15 minutes beforehand.

An Inquest was opened by the Coroner, Mr Robert Harvey, on 28th September 1891, held at St Matthew's School, Chester Street, Leicester. Given the evidence suggested that John was pushed in the canal, the Coroner adjourned the case, so that further evidence could be gathered. The second hearing of the Inquest was held 13th October 1891. As no further evidence was forthcoming an 'Open' verdict was recorded.

The Leicester Coroner's Office have no documents in their Archives, however, the articles in the 'Supplement to The Leicester Chronicle', dated 3rd Oct 1891 & 17th Oct 1891, record the details of the hearings.

John Ernest Thompson was buried 30th September 1891.

Woodier, John (1841? - 1921)

John Woodier was born in Coventry, Warwickshire, in approx 1841.
In January 1863 John, who was now a Ribbon Weaver, married Julia Farmer, in Coventry.
In 1870 John, Julia and their four children moved from Coventry to Leicester. The children, aged seven to one year old, were baptised in the Parish of Stoke, Warwickshire in January 1870.

The censuses from 1861 to 1901 show John's various occupations as Ribbon Weaver, Elastic Webb Weaver, Shop Keeper, Tube(?) Dresser and Gardener. The 1911 Census states no occupation.

By 1901 the family had moved to the Abbey Lane area.

John died in February 1921 aged 79. He was buried 1st March 1921.

Woodier, Julia (1843? - 1909)

Julia Farmer was born in Coventry, Warwickshire, round about 1843. She was the maternal Grandmother of John Ernest Thompson.

The 1861 Census shows she was a Silk Picker.

In January 1863 Julia married John Woodier, in Coventry.

In 1870 John, Julia and their four children moved from Coventry to Leicester.

By 1871 the census shows that Julia had become a Silk Winder. However that is the last census which records an occupation for Julia, but she did have a total of ten children.

Before her death the family had moved to 281 Abbey Lane, Leicester.

Julia died December 1909 aged 66. She was buried 16th December 1909, joining her young grandson, John Ernest Thompson, 1891 aged four years. Her husband John would join her in 1921 aged 79 years and Eliza Calvert her daughter in 1950 aged 78 years.

Guilford, George (1827 - 1891)

George Guilford was born in 1827 in Theddingworth and by the 1851 Census he was lodging at Enderby.

He was a Gentleman's Gardener in 1861 in Bradford and sometime between this date and the census of 1871 he moved to live in Leicester, but still as a gardener.

On 23rd June 1852 he married Harriett Winson, who lived in Enderby until her marriage.

Their daughter Florence was born in 1871 in Leicester and she worked in the shoe industry as a fitter. They are also the parents of John Thomas Guilford *(see Plot D349)*

Our contributor believes that George worked for the Winstanley family at Braunstone Hall, as a gardener.

From 1891 they lived in Lexham Street, Belgrave.

George died in August 1891 aged 63 years.

Guilford, Harriett (1830? - 1907)

Harriett Winson was born in Thurlaston around 1830 and lived in Enderby until her marriage to George Guilford on 23rd June 1852.

They moved into Lexham Street, Belgrave, and they had a daughter, Florence in 1871 and she eventually worked in the shoe industry as a Fitter. George and Harriett are also the parents of John Thomas Guilford *(see Plot D349)*.

Harriett died in January 1907 aged approximately 77 years, and was laid to rest in Belgrave Cemetery on 26th January 1907 with her husband George who died in August 1891 aged 63 years at Lexham Street and their daughter Florence who died in November 1905 aged 34 years. Both Harriett and Florence were living at 244 Willow Street at the time of their deaths.

Peel, Mary Ellen (1861 - 1960)

Mary Ellen Mould was born in 1861 at Skeffington, Leicestershire, daughter of Catherine and Henry Mould and one of a large family, which in the 1871 Census consisted of Walter, George Wallace, Kate, Ellen, Emily and Wade. all living in Skeffington Vale, Billesdon, Leicestershire.

By the 1881 Census the family had moved in the intervening years to 19, Bath Street, Belgrave, father Henry classing himself as a Laundry Proprietor, and Mary Ellen, called Ellen in the census was now 20 years old and working as a Laundress, (presumably for her father).

We then lose sight of Mary Ellen and her family on the census and the family pick up on her again with her married name of Peel.

Her husband, Mr Peel (first name unknown) was at some point landlord of the Lord Lyon public house on Thurcaston Road, Belgrave, and was at sometime a jockey. A picture of his horse called "Little Fanny" hung outside the pub for many years.

Mary Ellen died, aged 99, in August 1960 in Hillcrest Hospital, Leicester, (a scary, grim place in those days) and was laid to rest with her mother Catherine Mould who died in November 1883, aged 52 years, her father Henry Mould

Mary Ellen on her 99th birthday

who died in June 1919, aged 89 years and one of her brothers Walter who died in November 1941, aged 86 years.

Weston, Amy Mary (1868 - 1933)

Amy Mary Gibbs was born on 17th August 1868, in Northampton, the daughter of a builder and she married John Henry Wood Weston on 13th April 1903, six months after the death of his first wife, Frances.

Amy soon gave John three children, all girls, Ella May 1905, Kathleen Mary 1906 and Irene Frances in 1908. But soon tragedy was to strike the family when John Henry died suddenly of heart failure on 17th June 1909, after only six years of marriage.

Amy was, however, well provided for although she left the recently completed house, "Glenshee" in Manor Road, Oadby, (now known as "The Coppice" and part of the Leicester University), and moved with her family into "The Homestead", London Road, where she brought up her family and where she eventually died of cancer on 26th May 1933 aged 65 years.

She did however live to see two of her daughters married, Ella and Kathleen and her first grand daughter, Eileen Frances born in 1931.

Amy is laid to rest with John Henry and his first wife Frances, also John and Amy's eldest daughter Ella Amy, who, having married into the Owen family in 1928 died at the young age of 42 on 24th December 1947 at a home for incurables in Leamington Spa, suffering an illness similar to Multiple Sclerosis.

Weston, Frances Emma (1854 - 1902)

Frances Emma Walker was born in 1854 at Tugby, and married John Henry Wood Weston on 18th February 1879 at St Thomas a Becket Church, Tugby, Leicestershire.

John and Frances moved to Leicester, allowing John to build up his business, in 1881 living at 158 High Cross Street, with three men and a boy as employees. John, in the 1881 Census describes his occupation as a cabinet maker.

By 1891 they had moved to 40 Bruin Street, Belgrave and Frances was working as an upholsterer. Also living with them at this time was her father, George Walker who was a boot maker, aged 65 years.

By 1901, John and Frances had moved yet again to 314 Harrison Road, Belgrave.

There were no children by this marriage and Frances died suddenly at Harrison Road of heart failure on 3rd September 1902. John bought the burial plot in Belgrave Cemetery and erected the memorial. There was an inquest into Frances's sudden death, but the family have been unable to trace any reports or paperwork about it.

Weston, John Henry Wood (1851 - 1909)

John Henry was born on 16th June 1851, and was baptised John Henry Wood Weston, sixth son of Thomas and Clementina Wood of Ipstones in North Staffordshire.

John had moved to Fradswell, working as a cowman to his elder brother Joseph of Sun Farm. Although close to his brother, John Henry soon thought that Leicester offered better opportunities to work with his other brothers although Joseph visited him often in Leicester.

John Henry was soon working with older brother William Edwin who was a builder and a cabinet maker and he and John began to trade as Weston Bros. of 20 Duns Lane and later at 27 East Bond Street, the firm still being there in 1904.

John Henry married Frances Emma Walker at Tugby on 18th February 1879 still giving his occupation as cabinet maker. There were no children by this marriage.

Living and working in Leicester, by 1881 John was employing three men and a boy. By the next census they had moved to Belgrave, John giving his occupation as cabinet manufacturer.

In the 1890s John had joined with William Henry Winterton (who owned steam driven sawmills at 37 Upper Charles Street) to construct a large building to house equipment for making bricks.

In 1901, John and Frances had moved again and were living at 314 Harrison Road, Belgrave, Leicester, John now gave his occupation as brick manufacturer.

On the 3rd September 1902, Frances died of heart failure at home on Harrison Road and was buried at Belgrave Cemetery on the 6th September.

Six months later John Henry married Amy Mary Gibbs at the parish church of St. Sepulchre, Northampton on 13th April 1903. Amy was thirty five, a spinster of no occupation living at 23 Bailiff Street, Northampton.

Very soon there were three daughters born to the couple.

Unfortunately, on 17th June 1909, aged 58, John Henry died of heart failure at his newly built home "Glenshee", Manor Road, Oadby. (Glenshee is now part of the Leicester University and renamed "The Coppice" having been enormously enlarged and unrecognisable as the pleasant house John had built for his family).

John Henry is buried with his first wife, Frances Emma, his second wife, Amy Mary, whom he married 6 months after losing Frances and his first born daughter, Ella Amy, who died on 24th December 1947 aged 47, all in Belgrave Cemetery.

Hughes, Ann (1864 - 1940)

Ann Stanford was born in 1864, the daughter of Thomas Stanford from Wolverhampton and Hephzibah née Boden from Tipton, Staffordshire.

She had five siblings, John W. born 1862, Walter, born 1868, Frank, born 1871 and Ada, born 1875.

Ann met John Augustus Hughes in Wednesbury where he was employed as a brass finisher.

They were married in Spring 1886 and later had four children one of which was Nora Hughes, born 1896 *(See Nora Tomlinson Plot C277)*. There was also Albert S., born 1887, Walter Augustus, born 1892, and Doris, born 1894.

Although it isn't certain, it would appear that they moved to Leicester between 1911 and 1923.

Ann died on 5th February 1940 aged 76 years.

Ann with husband, John Augustus

Hughes, John Augustus (1865 - 1937)

John Augustus was the son of a blacksmith and was born in Manchester in 1865. Later his family were to move to Birmingham.

At the age of sixteen he was employed as a brass finisher in Wednesbury, where he met Ann Stanford who he married in the Spring of 1886 and they had four children, two boys and two girls including Nora, who was later to go to Oldham to work in the cotton mills, there meeting Walter Hamlet Tomlinson. *(See Plot C277)*

Little more is known about John Augustus, but at sometime it is thought that he travelled to France, and from his photograph there is a very becoming suave French look about him.

In the 1911 Census, John is listed as an Engineering Brass Worker, living at 47, Three Shires Oak Road, Smethwick, a private house with six rooms. His wife is not in employment, but son Walter Augustus is a nineteen year old waiter, Doris works as a Post Office Clerk and Nora is a dressmaker assistant. Quite a diverse set of occupations.

Between 1911 and 1923, the family had moved to Leicester, and John Augustus died at 69 Marston Road, Gipsy Lane, Belgrave on 5th January 1937 aged 71 years. He was laid to rest at Belgrave Cemetery and was joined by his wife Ann on 5th February 1940 aged 76 years. She too was living at the Marston Road address when she died.

📖

Foulds, Arthur (1870 - 1944)

Arthur was born on 17th March 1870 in Leicestershire.
He married twice, firstly to Mary Beck, formerly Winker, née Griffiths in 1900 and they lived at 33 Whatton Lodge, St Ives Road, Leicester.
After Mary's death in 1935, Arthur married a Mrs French of Naseby Road, Leicester.
He worked on the railways and died of a stroke in 1944, aged 74 years.

Foulds, Mary (1868 - 1935)

Mary Griffiths was born in Stafford in 1868.
She married three times, firstly to a Mr Winker, then a Mr Beck and finally in 1900 to Arthur Foulds.
When living in Leicester, Mary cooked for gentry and later assisted a local doctor to deliver babies.
Mary died aged 67 in 1935 of liver failure.

King, Hazel (1934 - 2009)

Hazel Sumner was born on 2nd December 1934 at 38 Essex Road, Leicester and was the youngest daughter of William Sumner and Agnes Foulds.
Hazel attended Wyvern Avenue Infant School, Northfield House Junior School and finally Alderman Newton Girls' School.
Hazel's first job was office work on Blackbird Road, then a clerical position with Frears and Black's Bakery, a shorthand typist at Eaton of Canada in Leicester and finally Hazel became head of office at a waste material firm in Sileby, mainly involving book-keeping
Hazel's hobbies included caravanning, needlework and making her own clothes.
She married Alan King on 25th August 1979 but sadly he died on 28th August 2007.
Hazel passed away at the Leicester Royal Infirmary from cancer on 24th November 2009 and her funeral took place at Gilroes Crematorium on 4th December.

Sumner, William (1894 - 1943)

William was born in Wellingore, Lincolnshire in May 1894.
Initially he worked on the land, and then during the First World War he served in the cavalry.

After the war he came to Leicester in search of employment and eventually found work in a foundry as a fettler, but hated the job.

William married Agnes Emily Foulds in 1928 and they had two daughters, Marcia and Hazel.

He enjoyed gardening, woodwork and taught himself to play the piano during the air raids of World War II.

William would take his family to Wellingore every Easter holiday to see his parents and they also went on holiday to the seaside every year.

Sadly, in 1943, whilst William was fetching his youngest daughter Hazel from her music lesson, he fell from his bicycle and hit his head on a kerbstone, causing a haemorrhage from which he died at the early age of 49 years.

William now rests with his mother-in-law Mary Foulds, who died in 1935, aged 67 years, and his father-in-law Arthur Foulds, who died in 1944 aged 74 years. The ashes of his daughter, Hazel King, who died in 2009, aged 74 are also in the grave.

Crofts, Hannah (1874 - 1944)

Hannah Barnett was born to William and Mary Barnett at Norton in the Moors, Staffordshire, in 1874. She was the third of six children.

Her father, William was a coal miner and died young and Mary, her mother, was left to bring up the children alone.

When Hannah was 14 years old, she went into domestic service as a maid to two maiden ladies, Caroline and Sarah Ann Brindley, 'living on their own means' in Burslem, Staffordshire, staying with them until she was 17 years old.

When she was 18 she came to Leicester to find work, becoming a shoe finder and lodging in Coral Street, Belgrave, Leicester.

On July 31st 1897, she married William Frederick Crofts at the Wesleyan Chapel, Bishop Street, Leicester.

William had been born and bred in Belgrave as were his thirteen siblings. He and Hannah set up home at 77 Down Street, but later moved to the Narborough Road area, returning to Glendon Street, Belgrave in the 1920s.

Hannah and William were both tee-total and members of the Rechabites. To become a member, a pledge was signed to abstain from drinking alcohol. Members paid a sum to this organisation each week which enabled the member to draw sick pay if out of work due to illness. *(See picture of a Rechabite march overleaf)*

On June 1st 1902, John William was born to Hannah and William. He was to be their only child.

In 1915, when Hannah's husband William was 39 years old, he joined the Leicestershire Regiment to fight in the Great War. Hannah and her son John didn't see him again for three years.

Hannah was laid to rest in Belgrave Cemetery on December 23rd 1944, aged 71 years, William's ashes are scattered elsewhere, as he wished.

Hannah's mother-in-law and father-in-law, Charles and Sarah Crofts, are also laid to rest in Belgrave Cemetery. *(See Plot C220)*

This photograph of the Rechabite marchers is believed to have been taken in Granby Street,
Leicester, with the march travelling towards the station.
Hannah is in the middle of the picture in her Sunday best (dark skirt, white blouse)
The Rechabites were based in Dover Street, in the old Baptist Church, later to become The Little Theatre

Bradford, John Henry (1887 - 1967)

John Henry (Jack) was born in Norwich in October 1887 and named after his father, John Henry. His mother was Ellen Bradford. He eventually moved to Leicester with his parents, who lived to be 100 and 101.

John Henry with his wife, Maud Elizabeth *(left)* and daughter Maud *(right)*

Jack married Maud Elizabeth Allen during the first three months of 1910 and lived at 101, Melrose Street in Leicester for the rest of his married life, and actually died in the same house.

He had one daughter, Maud, named after her mother, born later in 1910.

On the 1911 Census he listed himself as a Compositor at a general printers and one of Maud's female relations, Ada Allen was living at their home too. She is listed as a Hose Mender in a hosiery manufacturers.

He worked as a Lithographic Printer at the Co-operative Printers in Churchgate – he was a Master Printer and taught this skill at a college in Leicester two evenings a week until he was in his late 70's. He was known in his family as a man who worked very hard and lived for his job.

In his younger days he was keen on motorbikes and in 1923 he bought a Raleigh Combination 3 speed – an all chain-drive motorbike for the princely sum of £89.12s.6d., from a company called Kerr Bros, 9 Lower Redcross Street, Leicester. (The original invoice is still held by family)

When attempting to drive up Wardley Hill, the bike could only get a quarter of the way up and his wife Maud, who was on the back of the bike had to push it to the top.

Jack died on 27th January 1967 aged 80 years.

Bradford, Maud Elizabeth (1887 - 1962)

Maud was born in Leicester on 5th November 1887 and had two sisters who both died when quite young. She married Jack Bradford and they had one daughter, also named Maud.

Maud Elizabeth didn't go out to work as far as the family are aware, but did engage in "outwork" at her home. This involved Maud having a shoe machine in the back bedroom of her terraced house in Melrose Street. This was a very big, heavy piece of equipment which had a treadle worked by using her feet and when in use the vibration from it was very noisy. The family are not sure exactly what the process was called on this machine but it involved fitting the shoe onto a "last" and then machining a part of the shoe "upper" but not the sole.

During the Second World War, Maud cared for her granddaughter Corinne whilst her own daughter went out to work. In reality, she brought Corinne up in her most formative years. Corinne remembers that her Grandma was quite an unhappy lady, but gave Corinne a very good start in life during the war years.

Maud Elizabeth died on 19th April 1962 aged 74 years.

Pugh, Henry (1915 - 2000)

Henry Pugh (Harry) was born in Leicester in the Highfields area on the 8th April 1915. He was one of 14 children, seven boys and seven girls and his mother died in her early 40s. His father fought in the Great War and when discharged was suffering from "shell shock".

Harry was brought up in poverty. As a young boy he was expected to push a hand cart across the city to where his father kept pigs – this was every morning before he went to school. He had a very hard and poor up-bringing.

There was no such thing as "having a bath" in those days. Each of the fourteen children were washed, one after the other "in the kitchen copper". This was after the clothes washing had been done. These were very hard times.

Harry left home at 15 and went to live with an older sister. He wanted to be a butcher and managed to get employment with Bill Pegg (Butcher), who had a shop at the corner of Melrose Street.

He then met Maud Bradford jnr whom he later married.

Eventually he went to work in a butchers shop at 74 Belgrave Road run by a lady, Mrs Gentner. When war broke out, he was called up to join the R.A.F. He spent most of the war first in Ireland and then in Germany. He was a cook for the whole of this period, and was away for seven years with only short breaks at home. During this time, Maud gave birth to Corinne and on his return from the war he went back to the butchers shop and Mrs Gentner sold the business to him in 1946. The shop was re-named Harry Pugh (Family Butcher) and was his pride and joy. He slaughtered most of the meat himself and brought the business on from strength to strength. He ran it until 1973 and it was a sad day for him when it closed, but times were changing on Belgrave Road and the Asian culture was present with differing requirements.

He had a happy retirement and enjoyed his time with his two children and four grandchildren. However his life had been his business, he loved it, and everyone loved and respected him.

Harry died on 7th May 2000 aged 85 years.

Garner, Anne (1850 - 1954)

When Anne Garner died on 15th January 1954 aged 103 years she was the oldest person at that time to be laid to rest in Belgrave Cemetery.

Anne, to everyone in Belgrave who knew her, was known as "Granny Garner" and was without doubt a very determined lady, as the photograph of a painting executed during an earlier year of her life shows.

Anne Pickering was born in Leicester at 12 Caroline Street, on 28th May 1850, daughter of Thomas Pickering and his wife Elizabeth Pickering née Flowers and she started work at the age of nine for 2/6d a week (a little over 12 pence in today's money), as a Downstairs Maid.

She married Reuben Garner, a Shoe Riveter, in 1873. She had three sons and at the time of her 99th birthday, the family had increased to 19 grandchildren and 33 great grand-children still living.

During her lifetime she worked at various inns around Leicester as a domestic servant and in her final years she was in service as a Housekeeper to various Lord Mayors of the City of Leicester. In her later years she was determined to carry on working until she was 100 years old – which she achieved!

Just before her 100th birthday, and after expressing a desire to meet Prime Minister Clement Attlee and Mrs Attlee, a home visit was arranged by the local Labour Party during Mr Attlee's election tour, after which he gave a public address at the Corn Exchange, Leicester before the General Election. The following September "Granny" donned her coat and walked to the polls to cast her vote.

On "Granny's" 103rd birthday she was visited by Alderman Charles Keene and was looking forward to the Queen Elizabeth's coronation festivities, as a street party was arranged and she was to be the honoured guest.

"Hard work keeps me happy. Up at seven in the morning, do my own housework and back to bed at eight in the evening" was her recipe for a long life.

The only thing Anne disliked about being 100, was that people passing her terraced home stopped to look through her front room window. "They have no manners," she complained.

Anne outlived Reuben, who died 20th January 1926 aged 78 years. She may have lived longer, but she was very house proud and she had a fall whilst white-washing the coal cellar steps breaking her hip. Without the benefits of today's modern surgery, Anne died on 15th January

1954 and is laid to rest with Reuben and their daughter Henrietta Carter, who died aged 61 on 31st December 1935. They are all buried together in Belgrave Cemetery.

Crofts, Charles (1842 - 1898)

Charles Crofts was born to Benjamin and Elizabeth Crofts in Hinckley, sometime around 1842.

He married Sarah Dilley in the summer of 1861 and moved to Leicester, looking for work as a bricklayer.

They lodged first in Metcalf Street, but by the 1881 Census they had moved to 120 Dorset Street, Belgrave, and later still in 1891 the family were at 36 Moira Street.

He and Sarah had fourteen children, one of whom was William F. Crofts, born 1877, who later married Hannah, née Barnett, *(see Hannah Crofts Plot C5)*.

Charles appears to have worked very hard as he appears on the 1851 Census as a Bricklayer and by the 1881 Census he is listed as 'Builder employing 8 men and 1 boy'.

Charles died in June 1898 aged 56 years.

Crofts, Sarah (1844 - 1886)

Sarah Dilley was born in Hinckley in 1844, where she married Charles Crofts in 1861. Both she and Charles moved to Leicester looking for work, he in the building trade and she in hosiery.

Sarah had fourteen children, one of whom was William F. Crofts, born 1876, who later married Hannah, née Barnett, *(see Hannah Crofts Plot C5)*.

The rest of the children were Benjamin (1863), Sarah (1864), Mary A.M. (1865), Emma (1) (1866 died at 10 months old), John (1867), Charles (1869), Emma (2) (1870), Susan (1872), William, (1873, but died in February 1874), Florence E. (1875), Alice F. (1879), Lilian (1880), Robert (1881), Albert (1884).

Sarah died at the early age of 43 years in November 1886, and she is laid to rest in Belgrave Cemetery with Charles, who died in June 1898 aged 56 years. Also in the grave is Edith Mary Payne, who died in April 1921 aged 36 years. Edith was also related to the family.

Tomlinson, Norah (1896 - 1959)

Tomlinson, Walter Hamlet (1893 - 1942)

Nora Hughes was born on 10th February 1896 in Birmingham, one of four children born to John Augustus Hughes and his wife Ann née Stanford. John Augustus was born in Manchester, moved to Birmingham and met his wife Ann at Wednesbury. *(See Plot B33)*

Nora's siblings were Albert S Hughes, Doris Hughes, and Walter A Hughes.

On the 1911 Census, Nora is listed as a Dressmaker Assistant, aged 15 years, but she was later to move to Oldham to work in one of the cotton mills, meeting Walter Hamlet Tomlinson, an iron foundry worker, born in the summer of 1893 near Saddleworth, whom she later married in 1923.

Norah's family had moved to Leicester, living at 69 Marston Road, Belgrave, so she and Walter came down to be married at St. Michael and All Angels Church, situated on Melton Road, Belgrave, (now Sabras Radio).

Their honeymoon was "a lovely day on the River Soar." They hired a rowing boat for the day and then returned to 182 Acre Lane, Oldham, Lancashire, Walter to the iron foundry and Nora to the cotton mill.

Nora miscarried one child and later had a stillborn baby girl, but in 1933 they had a boy, John Edgar Tomlinson and moved to Leicester to be nearer Nora's family.

Walter had a job working in an iron foundry once again, where due to the poor working conditions, he contracted tuberculosis eventually dying in November 1942 aged 49 years.

Although only a boy of nine when his father died, John Tomlinson can still remember his distraught mother throwing herself across his bed saying "God thought better of it…"

Nora died in January 1959 of cancer aged 62 years.

Both Walter and Nora were living at 18 Huntingdon Road, Belgrave, Leicester at the time of their deaths.

Powell, John Barnett (1854 - 1923)

John Barnett Powell was born in Daventry in 1854. He was a veteran of the Second Afghan War (1878 - 1880) and was awarded the Afghan Medal.

He was married to Sarah Anne Vines at St Mark's Church, Belgrave in 1882.

They had 17 children during their marriage although only 10 survived. Seven died at very early ages, months not years.

Their eldest son John who was married and lived in Dundee was a Petty Officer in the Royal Navy. He was lost at sea in HM Submarine D3 off the coast of France in 1918 aged 30 years.

Their son-in-law, Charles Downward who was married to their eldest daughter Elizabeth, was also a Petty Officer in the Royal Navy and he was killed when HMS Princess Irene, a mine layer, exploded in the Medway Estuary, Kent, in 1915.

He was 32. Both of these sailors are mentioned in the Friends of Belgrave Cemetery Roll of Honour book.

John Barnett passed away in March 1923 aged 69 and Sarah Anne in September 1936, they were both living at 11 Roughton Street at the time of their deaths. They are both interred at Belgrave Cemetery, along with other members of the family;

Lilian May Powell aged two months, died July 1885, Charles Powell aged two years died March 1892, both were living at 41 Abbey Lane, Leicester when they died. Also Thomas Powell aged one year,

Sarah Anne Powell
(née Vines)

died September 1903 and Henry James Powell aged two months died September 1904 and both were living at 36 Flax Road when they died.

45

Squires, Lizzie (1861? - 1936)

It is not known for certain the date of Lizzie Hall's birth but on the 1911 Census she is listed as 50 years of age so 1861 is a rough calculation. Again little is known of her early life, although a member of Ancestry Family Tree has done some research and it is thought that maybe Lizzie had been married before with the surname 'Brown'. The family wonder if William George Squires, her husband, moved from Birstall where he was living before marriage, to Belgrave as Lizzie was already living there.

What is known is that William and Lizzie moved to Belgrave, where William entered the shoe trade.

They resided first in Claremont Street at number 4 and later on number 8, before moving to 24 Linford Street where they remained until their deaths.

Lizzie was to have seven children, six boys and a daughter, William, Olive Lizzie, Walter, Albert Edward, Herbert, Charlie and Edwin.

Olive Lizzie was born in 1895, and in the 1911 Census was a Shoe Machinist. She was to live to the grand age of 90 years.

Lizzie and William were to lose one son, Albert Edward who died in June 1899 aged one month.

Their eldest son William or 'Willie' Squires never married and continued to live at 24 Linford Street until his death on 27th March 1955, aged 65 years. Willie worked at the sewage farm with his father until he moved to a position as Grave Digger at Gilroes cemetery. He was a well-known member of the Checketts Road Working Mens' Club, holding a number of positions on the Committee.

Walter, the third child, was also a very well-known member and committee member of the Checketts Road WMC. He had a son called Morris, who was a football referee.

Herbert worked as a Roundsman for the Co-op Dairy, but gave up the job after one of the cart horses badly bit his hand. After that experience he hated horses, sticking to motorbikes, then cars! He was married late in his 40s to Mabel Snowden, the widowed landlady of 'The Hotel Belgrave', Loughborough Road. There were no children.

Charlie, born in 1903, needs more research but it is known he had three children.

Edwin 'Harold' was born in 1904 (and is the Grandfather of the contributor). He was employed by the Co-op Dairy for all of his working life, continuing to live in the Belgrave area. He had 4 children with his wife Elsie. He died in 1993 aged 86.

All six of Lizzie and William's surviving children lived into adulthood.

Lizzie not only brought up her family but it is noted in the 1911 Census she is also working as a charlady, obviously having to supplement the family income.

Lizzie died on 17th February 1932 aged approximately 75 years.

Squires, William George (1856 - 1944)

William George Squires was born in Birstall in October 1856. He lived with his parents and after leaving school he worked as a farm labourer.

After meeting Lizzie Hall, they moved to Belgrave and he took up employment in some of the many shoe firms in Leicester and around Belgrave, working as a Laster, Riveter and then a Finisher.

After a little over twenty years working in the shoe trade, William then gained employment as a Borough Labourer, working at a sewage farm until he retired.

He kept two allotments in Belgrave, and our contributor's father had fond memories of visiting his grandfather at the allotments.

They never left Belgrave, as their family grew they resided in two properties in Claremont Street, numbers 4 and 8, one after the other, before moving to 24 Linford Street where William and Lizzie remained until they died.

William George died on the 9th November 1944 aged 88 years and is buried with his wife Lizzie who had died on 17th February 1936 aged approximately 75 years and their baby son Albert Edward Squires, died 1899 aged one month.

Thompson, Charles (1863 - 1925)

Charles was born in 1863 at Tamworth, Stafford and worked as an Elastic Web Weaver, meeting his future wife Mary Ann Williamson at the same factory. They married on 25th December 1882 at St. Editha's Church, Tamworth, and moved to Leicester in 1898.

They had nine children, losing one son, Charles in the Great War in 1917. He was 27 years old and is buried at Bienville Cemetery, France.

The other children were Ada born 1885, William 1886, Elizabeth 1888, John 1891, Alfred 1898, Elsie 1901, Harry 1903 and Leonard born 1908.

Charles died in August 1925 in Leicester aged 62 years.

The Thompson Family
Back left to right: Alfred, John, Elizabeth, Charles *(killed in France, WWI)*
Middle left to right: Ada, Charles, Mary Ann, William
Front left to right: Harry, Elsie, Leonard

Thompson, Mary Ann (1864 - 1935)

Mary Ann Williamson was born in Tamworth, Stafford in 1864 and worked as an Elastic Web Weaver at a factory where she met Charles Thompson whom she married on 25th December 1882. They moved to Leicester in 1898, after their son Alfred was born and lived in the Humberstone Road area of Leicester.

Mary Ann had nine children but unfortunately one son, Charles, was killed in the Great War, in 1917.

Another son, Alfred also died at the very young age of 35.

The other children were three girls and four boys.

Mary Ann's husband Charles, died in August 1925 in Leicester and is laid to rest with Mary Ann, who died in June 1935 aged 71 years, and also their son Alfred, who died aged 35 years in 1933. (He was living at 25 Erskine Street, Leicester at the time.)

Also in the grave according to cemetery records is Alice Elizabeth Gillgask aged 4 years, who died in April 1892 at 24 Portland Street, Belgrave. Although she has no connection with the family, she is mentioned as a mark of respect.

Keeling, Percival Turney (1881 - 1941)

Percival was born in Heanor in Derbyshire in 1881.
He married Jane Kershaw, who was born on 29th December 1879 in Basford, Nottingham and was on all accounts a very quiet lady, on 7th February 1903 in Heanor.

Percival with wife Jane and children Walter and Florrie

In 1912 he was headhunted by McTafats, Dyers and Finishers of Hosiery in Aberdeen and took up his new position of assistant manager moving his family, wife Jane, son Walter and daughter Florrie to 37 Thistle Street, Aberdeen. He also carried out coast guard work along Aberdeen Docks during World War I.

While in Aberdeen, two more sons were born, Arthur in December 1915 and Albert in March 1920, the father of our contributor.

In 1921, Percival was head-hunted once more by Wolsey, Abbey Meadow Mills as foreman of the Dyeing and Finishing department, so all six members of the family moved from Aberdeen to live in Ross Walk, Belgrave and later on to move to Shaftesbury Avenue, Belgrave in Leicester.

Percival was quite lucky and in a competition run by the 'News of the World' he predicted the 1st, 2nd and 3rd winners in the Grand National. He was presented with a cheque for £500 at the opening of a city cinema (possibly the Odeon) in Leicester on 28th July 1932.

He used some of the money to buy the house next door in Shaftesbury Avenue, Belgrave to rent out.

He also had an allotment, which someone else looked after because he couldn't get his hands rough due to his work examining silk stockings, but he always collected the prizes! There is still a photograph in the family.

In 1941, his son Albert who was engaged on top secret war work on Radar with the R.A.F. in Ventnor, Isle of Wight, took a message that his father had died of pneumonia. Due to his important work in the war, Albert could not get home.

Percival died on 14th February 1941 aged 59 years. His wife Jane was to die on 23rd October 1951 aged 71 years. Both Percival and Jane were still resident at 36 Shaftesbury Avenue at the time of their deaths. They are both together in the cemetery.

Percival *(centre)* celebrates his win at Wolsey Ltd

Percival collecting another trophy - for his vegetables this time

📖

Beechey, Albert Ernest (1906 - 1985)

Albert Ernest Beechey was born on 26th December 1906 at 89 Melrose Street, Belgrave. He was called 'Jim' from an early age because he was such a cheerful individual hence 'Sunny Jim'. This name stayed with him throughout his life.

He was the sixth of a close family of eight children.

He married Rose Evelyn Hydon in 1928, and had three daughters, Valerie Rose, Barbara Caroline, Margaret Elizabeth.

He joined the Royal Welsh Fusiliers in 1941 and was wounded in 1944 during D-Day action. He was mentioned in dispatches for an act of bravery and was awarded the King's Medal and an army pension.

He was divorced from his first wife Rose in 1948, marrying Ivy Glover née Hales in 1950 and had a fourth daughter, Patricia Ann in the same year.

After the war he was employed at Rawson's on Evington Valley Road, in Leicester as a clicker in the shoe industry. He was a keen gardener, growing wonderful roses, vegetables and fruit in his much loved back garden at 360 Humberstone Lane. He was also a keen Leicester City supporter.

He was a very gentle man and was always very smartly dressed, even when gardening!

When his wife Ivy died in 1983 he lost interest in his garden, sport and even life. He died in the Leicester Royal Infirmary on 14th August 1985, aged 79 years, two weeks after a traffic accident on the road outside his beloved Humberstone Lane home.

Beechey, Ivy Irene (1912 - 1983)

Ivy Hales was born on 24th November 1912 at 111 Taylor Street. The eldest of five children, her father died in 1930 aged 39 years

She worked first in the hosiery trade as a Mender and then became a Shoe Machinist and married William George Glover in 1931 at Leicester Register Office. They set up home at 30 Tiverton Avenue, later moving to Humberstone Lane.

George was a Master Blacksmith and a well known character in horse circles. They both won many rosettes with their horse and trap at gymkhanas.

George died in 1949 and Ivy met Albert Beechey and they married in 1950, their daughter being born in the same year.

Ivy was a very positive person with a great sense of humour. She loved her home and family and was famed for her wonderful cookery skills.

Ivy died on 18th August 1983, aged 71 years.

Glover, William George (1907 - 1949)

William George Glover was born at 112 Melrose Street, Belgrave in 1907, the eldest of five children.

He became a Master Blacksmith and had his premises at 132a Highcross Street. He won a gold medal for his skills in horseshoe-making.

In 1931 he married Ivy Hales at the Leicester Register Office and set up home at 30 Tiverton Avenue, later moving to 360 Humberstone Lane, a bungalow with an acre of land.

They also owned a paddock at Keyham where their horse was stabled. They had a wonderful trap and made frequent appearances at gymkhanas, winning many rosettes for the appearance and behaviour of their horse team.

He was a well-known Leicester character in horse circles and was a very gentle man who was always smiling.

He died on 8th February 1949 at a fairly young age of 42, having bought his own grave plot and chosen his coffin of Redwood.

He is buried with Ivy, who died on 18th August 1983 aged 71 years and Ivy's second husband, Albert Ernest Beechey who died on 14th August 1985.

William George and Ivy with 'Brenda' and the trap

LARRATT, EDWARD (1874 – 1945)

LARRATT, SUSAN MARIA (1872 – 1942)

Born in 1874, Edward Larratt was the second child of Dennis and Ann Larratt née Bott. They had been married in 1871 at Loughborough. Dennis was a framework Knitter at this time.

Very little is known about Edward. He was the middle child, his sister Susan Maria was born in 1872 and his younger brother John in 1880. Along with Susan, he was to become a Framework Knitter too and, it seems that neither he nor Susan ever married.

When he was 16 in 1894 their father Dennis died. Their mother Ann had died in 1890, so the family were parentless at a early age. This may explain why Edward and Susan stayed together. Also Susan had a speech and hearing impediment from birth which no doubt made her quite reliant on her family.

Susan died in 1942 aged 70 years and Edward in 1945 aged 71 years.

How the paths of Edward Larratt and William George Glover crossed are not known, but at sometime after 1942 when Susan died aged 70 years and 1945 when Edward himself passed away, aged 71 years he had sold the grave deeds to William George, thus explaining the two families in the same grave plot.

Albert Ernest Beechey's ashes are buried at Belgrave Cemetery, with his wife Ivy who died on 18th August 1983 aged 71 years and her first husband William George Glover, who died on 8th February 1949 aged 42 years.

Also in the grave are Susan Maria Larratt, who died in November 1942 aged 70 years and Edward Larratt, who died in October 1945 aged 71 years, both of whom were living at 43 Acorn Street, Belgrave at the time of their deaths. *Although not part of the family, Susan and Edward are mentioned as a mark of respect)*

Black, Edith Ann (1880 - 1962)

Edith Ann was born in 1880 at 17 Palmer Street in Belgrave and lived with her father, Joseph, an Elastic Weaver and her mother Jane Foreman along with her six brothers and sisters. Little is known of what her employment was before she married which was sometime between 1901 and 1911 although in the 1901 Census she is described as a Shoe Fitter.

By 1911 she was living at 32 Thurcaston Road, Belgrave, and described as head of the house and employed as a Laundress. It was at this address where she brought up her family although the house has since been demolished.

Her children were Kate Lillian, Beatrice May and Ernie Victor. Unfortunately Edith was left a single mother when Kate was just seven years old.

Although alone, she managed to provide for and protect her children as much as possible in those difficult circumstances. Edith would take in laundry to earn money and Kate and Beatrice being older were expected to help out. The helping out would include them being awoken in the middle of the night to attend to the turning of the laundry.

The family were told that on occasion Edith was invited to have tea by the ladies who lived in Belgrave Hall (the Misses Ellis). Edith was a very strong, independent, dignified and kind lady and no doubt had made a great impression on the sisters, who as Quakers engaged in many kind and thoughtful deeds for the good of the less fortunate residents of the village of Belgrave.

Edith died on 8th August 1962 aged 82 years and is laid to rest with her younger sister Sarah Foreman who died on 6th April 1955.

There are three other people in this grave all with different names, Jessie Yates aged four months, Ruth Rudd aged three years, and Jane Jarvis aged 56 years.

The family do not know who these two children and adult were, but in days when there was little money available, maybe a kind hearted woman like Edith made space for families who couldn't afford to buy a grave plot, or did she buy the plot from another family? We may never know!

Holliland, Bertha (1873 - 1940)

Bertha Payne was born on 19th February 1873 in the Parish of St. Margaret's, Leicester. Her parents were James and Ann Payne.

Little is known about her early life but apparently she was a Shoe Fitter before marriage.

She married George Clipson Holliland on 30th March 1891 in Leicester and their first home was at 35½ Albion Hill, Leicester, and it would appear that she wasn't employed after she married.

Bertha and George had 9 children, 7 of whom survived.

Lilian Annie, was born on 7th May 1892 , followed by George James born on 7th December 1893 both born in Leicester.

Next came William born on 10th January 1895 in Leicester, and he was followed by Bertram born on 11th February 1897 at 67 Stanley Street, Leicester. Gladys Bertha followed him, born on 28th August 1900 in Leicester.

Bertha had a stillborn child in 1903 whilst living at 55 Acorn Street, Belgrave Leicester, and little Grace Caroline was born 1905 and died in the same year.

Two years later Arthur was born on 28th September 1907, and finally Alice Elizabeth was born on 4th May 1910, again both in Leicester.

Bertha died on 16th August 1940 aged 67 years.

Holliland, George Clipson (1872 - 1943)

George was born 24th June 1872 to William and Sarah Holliland née Clipson at 8 George Street, Leicester.

He married Bertha Payne on 30th March 1891, in Leicester and their first home was at 35½ Albion Hill, Leicester. They had nine children of which seven survived.

His occupation was a House Painter, and in the 1900s (presumably after the Great War), George worked for quite a while in Paris. Family oral history mentions him working with gold leaf.

George had a car and a chauffeur as well as putting his youngest daughter through private school, so it must have paid well!

Whilst living at 42 Acorn Street, he died on 30th July 1943 aged 71 years, when he fell from a ladder in Upper Kent Street, Leicester. He was badly injured and on arrival at Leicester Royal Infirmary he was pronounced dead.

It was a serious enough accident to merit inclusion in the Leicester Mercury.

He is laid to rest with his wife Bertha who died on 16th August 1940 aged 67 years.

Their 31 year old son Bertram, who was killed in a motorcycle accident in May 1928 also rests in Belgrave Cemetery *(in Plot C832)*.

Wylly, John Edwin (1878? - 1950)

John Edwin Wylly, known as Edwin as stated on his headstone, was born in Leicester about 1878.

On the 1901 Census he is noted as a Shoe Riveter in the boot and shoe industry, aged 23 and classed as single.

All that changed when he met Eliza Haines and they were married on 7th June 1902. She had come to Leicester to work in service from Langrick Ville in Lincolnshire where she was born.

On the 1911 Census, aged 33, John was working as a Drayman Fruiterer, and had three children. Eventually there were to be four daughters and a son, and the family were living in Down Street, Belgrave.

John is remembered with affection as a kind and funny Grandad, who was very family orientated and a Baptist church-goer who attended Carey Hall, on Catherine Street. He was to live all his life in Leicester.

One of his granddaughters says her mother can remember walking with him sometimes to take his horse to a field in the direction of Barkby Road, which in those days was not built on.

John Edwin was still living at 67 Down Street when he died on 19th November 1950 and is laid to rest in Belgrave Cemetery.

Wilkinson, Edith Evelyn (1898 - 1932)

Edith Evelyn Southwell was born to Arthur and Ada Southwell in 1898. Her father had been born in Wolverhampton and her mother in Leicester and they had married at St. Peter's Church, Belgrave, Leicester.

Edith had married a fruit salesman, George Baxter Wilkinson and it is thought by the present family she too married at St Peter's Church, Belgrave, like her parents. Her family were living at 121 Halkin Street, Belgrave, Leicester at this time.

Of her siblings, Edith had lost her older brother Leonard in the Great War, aged just nineteen, brothers Ernest and Henry both died in 1922 aged 16 and 21 respectively and her sister Doris in 1924 aged 22, all of whom contracted tuberculosis. In 1926 her father also died of the disease. They are all at rest in Belgrave Cemetery *(see Plot E892)*

George and Edith now had two children of their own.

The first born, Leonard George Wilkinson unfortunately died aged six months and was interred on 3rd May 1921. He was known as Guy as he had been born on 5th November 1921, and the burial plot was purchased for his burial. It is not known what caused the child's death.

Another child, Kathleen was born in January 1928, and is still alive.

Edith died of tuberculosis in the Sanatorium, Groby Road, Leicester, on 12th June 1932, aged 34 and she was laid to rest in Belgrave Cemetery on 16th June 1932 with Leonard George Wilkinson, her baby son.

Edith's husband George Baxter Wilkinson was to later remarry and worked as a Licensed Victualler in Cromer, Norfolk, where he died on 11th February 1970.

Edith with her husband, George Baxter Wilkinson and their daughter Kathleen

Moore, Leslie (1912 - 1942)

Leslie, eldest son of Lydia and Sidney Moore, and grandson of Thomas and Annie Darlaston, was born on 27th February 1912 at 6 Dundonald Road, Belgrave and was baptised on the 24th April 1912 at St. Mark's Church, Belgrave.

He was an office clerk with the B.U. (British United Shoe Machinery Company).

On 29th July 1937 he married Marjorie Guilford (daughter of Charles Thomas and Florence Guilford) at St. Michael and All Angels Church, Belgrave.

They lived at 67 Woodbridge Road, Belgrave.

On 7th November 1940 he enlisted into the Royal Army Service Corps (RASC), and he was in the Territorial Army, Unit 106 Bridge Coy.

Leslie with his wife Marjorie
1937

He went from Private to Corporal in just over two years.

On Saturday 19th December 1942, he was cycling along Braunstone Gate. He pulled out to avoid a stationary van and his front wheel got caught in a tram line. Leslie was thrown from his cycle in front of a Midland Red bus. He died of his injuries in the ambulance near the Royal Infirmary.

He is laid to rest in Belgrave Cemetery close to his grandfather and grandmother Darlaston, two sisters, Iris Nellie Moore, and Alma Kathleen Moore and his younger brother Dennis Moore whom he had tried to rescue from the canal in 1931. *(See Plot E776)*

HOLLILAND, BERTRAM (1897 - 1928)

Bertram was born on 11th February 1897 at 67, Stanley Street, Leicester to George and Bertha Clipson Holliland, both of whom are buried in Belgrave Cemetery *(see Plot No C548)*

By 1901 the family were living in Bruin Street, George employed as a House Painter and Bertha as a Shoe Fitter.

At this time, Bertram had two sisters, Lilian born 1892 and Gladys born 1901 and also two brothers, George, born in 1893 and William born 1895.

By the 1911 census they were living at 42 Acorn Street, Belgrave and Bertram was employed as a Barber's Apprentice.

Bertram married Lilian Pywell in 1914 and they went on to have four children.

Bertha, born 27th December 1914 at the Maternity Hospital, Causeway Lane, Leicester, Eric Douglas, born 28th August 1919 at Leicester (he died on 21st June 1970 in the General Hospital), Gladys, born 28th August 1921 and Joyce, born in 1923.

Unfortunately Bertram died on 30th May 1928 aged 31 years following a motorcycle combination accident.

Bertram, who was living at 27 Bath Street when he died, rests at Belgrave Cemetery.

These details are from the Cemetery records and there is some uncertainty as to whether they are related to the Holliland family but are included out of respect: Albert Edward Flewitt, died 6th September 1893 aged 24 years, Edward Cousins, died 31st October 1896 aged 21 years, both living at 42 Newington Street, Belgrave and Annie Stone died 27th January 1939 aged 76 years of 287 Catherine Street, Leicester.

Mason, John Henry (1871 - 1938)

John Henry Mason was born in Grantham, Lincolnshire in 1871, to an Iron Founder, Samuel Mason and his wife Sarah Mason.

He was the second son and by 1881 Samuel's family consisted of Thomas Wills, born 1869, Emma born 1874, Arthur born 1876 and Florence, born in 1879.

Samuel's sister Martha was also residing with them at the time. She was stated on the census form as a cotton spinner born in Coventry in 1835.

After leaving school, John Henry became a member of the family iron foundry business, which had been started by Samuel, his father, in Allington Street, off Brandon Street, Belgrave, joining his brother Thomas Wills Mason. Thomas is buried in Welford Road Cemetery.

John Henry was married to Minnie Wells, in the spring of 1891. There were two sons of the marriage, Bert and Ernest.

This photograph shows John Henry driving his family in car registration number BC57

Tragically Bert was killed in action, aged 27 years on 16th November 1918 and he is mentioned on the memorial at Belgrave but buried in Mikra British Cemetery, Kalamaria, Greece.

John Henry's wife Minnie died on 14th February 1936 aged 66 years and John Henry died on 14th February 1938 aged 67 years. John and Minnie were residing at 93 Loughborough Road, Belgrave at the time of their deaths.

Mason, Arthur (1878 - 1925)

Arthur Mason was born in 1878 and worked on the management side of the family iron foundry business which had been started by his father Samuel and was run from premises in Allington Street, (off Brandon Street), Belgrave. Samuel was a very successful business man and owned a great deal of property in the Belgrave area which he rented out.

Arthur married Edith Laura Wilby in the summer of 1897.

There were three children born to them, Cecil Victor Arthur Mason, born 1898, Arthur Ronald Mason (jnr), born 1902 and Clement Samuel Mason (Clem), born 1903. Cecil Victor always hated his name and usually called himself Cyril.

Arthur Mason snr died in June 1925 aged 47 years.

Arthur and his family are seen in the motor car registration BC 56
The child nearest the camera is Cecil Victor, his brother Clement Samuel and Arthur jnr
The photo was taken about 1906

Mason, Clement Samuel (1903 – 1950)

Clement Samuel Mason was born in 1903, his parents being Arthur and Edith Laura Mason.

Known as Clem, he worked as an electrical maintenance engineer at Belgrave Pumping station for many years and at the time of his death was living in Stonehill Avenue, Birstall.

He was laid to rest with his parents in March 1950.

Mason, Edith Laura (1875 - 1931)

Edith Laura Wilby was born in 1875, her father owning a chemist business in Humberstone Road, Leicester.

She married Arthur Mason in the summer of 1897.

Edith can also be seen sitting in motor car registration BC 56 in the picture on the previous page.

Edith died in June 1931, aged 56 years, joining her husband, Arthur who had died in June 1925 aged 47 years. They were both residing at 89 Loughborough Road, Belgrave at the time of their deaths. They were to be joined by their son Clement in March 1950 aged 46 years.

Edith Laura and Arthur Mason
with eldest son Cecil Victor

Billington, John Thomas (1908 - 1935)

Born in 1908, the son of John William and Elizabeth Fanny Billington, by all accounts from the Billington family, Jack, as he was known by everyone, was a lovely man with everything to live for. He had a lovely smile, which used to be commented on.

He married Gladys Miles sometime at the end of 1933, but when she was three months pregnant he contracted cancer and in a very short time died on 4th August 1935 aged 27 years having never seen his son, who was named Jack, after his father.

John Thomas is buried at Belgrave with his wife Gladys, who died on 9th August 1988, aged 80 years.

Toach, Gladys (formerly Billington) (1908 - 1988)

Gladys Miles was born in Leicester in 1908 and married John Thomas Billington, known as Jack to his family, sometime in the autumn of 1933. *(They are pictured above)*

After his death from cancer at the very young age of 27 years, she gave birth to Jack in the autumn of 1935. Some time lapsed and eventually Gladys remarried becoming Gladys Toach. Gladys died on 9th August 1988 aged 80 years.

Smith, Hannah (1884 - 1965)

Hannah Gaskin was born in Mildenhall near Cambridge in 1884. One of thirteen children, Hannah had ten brothers and two sisters. She was a member of the travelling community but little is known about her life before she married Noah Smith, nor when and where they were married.

Hannah Smith *(right)* with eldest daughter Jane at a family wedding

At first they lived at 159 Bardolph Street, Belgrave, where Hannah gave birth to her eldest daughter Jane on 19th March 1912. Eventually there would be Robert, Noah, Jane, Sally, Frances, Elizabeth and Dorothy. Two of her children, James and Sidney died in infancy and are laid to rest in Belgrave Cemetery with Boy Gaskin, Hannah's brother in Plot E243.

Later Hannah moved with the family to 117 Highcross Street, Leicester, where she ran a shoe shop, and Noah dealt in horse breaking and dealing.

Our contributor remembers, "My grandmother was a petite Victorian lady, very strict but fair, always at home to welcome my brother and I when we walked home from school together. Sometimes I wonder just what Grandmother would think of the world we live in today. I can still remember her remark that a loaf of bread would be a shilling (5 pence) before they were done!

Would she believe it is now over a pound!"

Hannah died on 10th March 1965 aged 81 years, at home in Melton Mowbray surrounded by her family.

The numerous family members filled seventeen Rolls Royce cars for the drive to St Mark's Church, Belgrave for the funeral service, after which Hannah was laid to rest with her husband Noah.

Smith, Jane (1912 - 1960)

Jane was born to Noah and Hannah Smith on 19th March 1912, their eldest daughter.

When Hannah and Noah's daughter Dorothy, seen *(left)* with Jane, was deserted by her husband in 1947, Jane offered to help her youngest sister to raise her two young children.

Jane was true to her word, living with them and helping with the upbringing of her niece and nephew. Unfortunately she died after a short illness on 9th November 1960, aged 48 years.

Dorothy Marshall took on the role of chairperson of the Friends of Belgrave Cemetery as a tribute to this kind, caring woman.

When they were children her beloved aunt, Jane, was always there with a hug and a kiss to soothe away Dorothy and her brother John's tears. Her aunt's values and selfless devotion to family duty were to set Dorothy and her brother along the road to adult life.

Jane is laid to rest with her father, Noah Smith and her mother, Hannah.

Smith, Noah (1879 - 1960)

Noah Smith was born in Caunton, near Southwell, Nottinghamshire in 1879. There are no details of when or where he married Hannah Gaskin but they lived at 159 Bardolph Street, Belgrave for a time.

Noah Smith seated *(right)*

Noah inherited his love of horses from his father, Bob Smith. As a child, our contributor remembers being taken to what her grandfather spoke of as "The Block", really the Horse Repository, in the Charles Street, Lee Street area of Leicester, with a cobble stone area for the horses to be run up and down, the horses in the stalls and the auctioneer up high above her. To a small girl it was an impressive sight.

Noah was one of the last of the old horse dealers in the Midlands. He had attended almost every market at Melton and Leicester for well over fifty years, breaking in horses for many famous people in the area.

Among his close friends were winning show-jumpers Ted Williams and Pat Smythe.

Later Noah and Hannah, moved to 117 Highcross Street, Leicester, where Hannah ran a shoe shop, and her daughter Dorothy always spoke of the high leg boots that she and her four sisters wore, and never forgot the time she was allowed to ride her pony to Elbow Lane school. The trouble was she did not know that having ridden the poor pony down the narrow entry it could not reverse out!

Noah also had fields on Blackbird Road and at Syston, and in those days it was a common sight to see fifty or so of his horses roaming loose in the street near his home.

Later they moved to Rookery Lane, Thurmaston where he lived until his death on 26th March 1960, aged 81 years, his funeral taking place on 31st March 1960 at St. Mark's Church, Belgrave.

The cortège of twelve gleaming Rolls-Royces were crammed into the narrow Rookery Lane at Thurmaston.

Floral tributes were many and of great ingenuity. A floral grey mare complete with trap sat on the roof of one hearse; another carried a vacant chair set before the hearth, modelled in flowers. Many mourners had travelled sixty or seventy miles to attend with Hannah and her remaining two sons and five daughters. It must have been quite a sight.

Noah was laid to rest in Belgrave Cemetery where his eldest daughter Jane joined him 8 months later in November 1960 aged 48 years and his wife Hannah five years later in March 1965 aged 81.

Noah and Hannah's daughter Sally and husband William (Billy) Elliott are also laid to rest in section D.

Noah and Hannah's third daughter, Frances and her husband John Sidney Charles Bennett are laid to rest in Section C.

Cramp, Ada (1871 - 1963)

Ada Moore, born in June 1871 was the daughter of Nodous and Susanna Moore, and sister of Clara, Lily, Florence, James and Walter.

She married James Cramp at St. Leonard's Church, Leicester in April 1895. James was a coal dealer.

Ada and James lost a daughter who was drowned at the wharf in Leicester.

Ada worked as a cleaner at the B.U. (British United Shoe Machinery Company) in Belgrave, and even when into her 90's she walked into Leicester twice a week.

She lived and died at 34 Olphin Street in 29th August 1963 (a week before her great nephew was married) at the grand age of 92 years.

Ada Cramp

Moore, Clara (1869 - 1955)

Moore, Lily (1883 - 1971)

Clara was born in October 1869, the daughter of Nodous and Susanna Moore and sister to Ada, Lily, Florence Ann, James and Walter Moore.

Born in March 1883, Lily was Clara's younger sister.

They were both originally in the hosiery trade, Clara working at R. Rowley as a Linker.

According to Kelly's Directory, Clara owned a draper's shop at 3 Belgrave Road from 1922 until at least 1928. Both sisters had strong views on abstaining from alcohol.

In 1932 Clara and her sister moved to 26 Melton Road, Belgrave, where they either rented or managed a draper's shop 'Moore's Babywear'.

Clara Moore
1899

Lily Moore

At first they both lived above the shop but then went to live on the new Walker Road estate in Birstall, whilst still running the shop until their retirement.

Clara died on 7th July 1955 aged 85 years.

Lily died on 14th April 1971, aged 88 years, and was laid to rest with her sister Clara on 20th April 1971 and Ada Cramp née Moore, who died on 29th August 1963 aged 92.

Lily & Clara
1949

Jackson, Annie Elizabeth (1863 - 1932)

Annie Elizabeth Carr was born on 15th February 1863 in Hunslet, Yorkshire, and was one of ten children.

She worked as a Woollen Cloth Weaver and on Christmas Day 1889 she married Walter Jackson, a Carpenter.

In total, Annie had four sons, Albert, Joseph, Arthur and Wilfred and three girls, Ada, Lillian and Gertrude, all born in Hunslet. *(Annie is shown opposite with her family)*

At sometime between 1901 and 1905 they moved down to Leicester and into a new home in Melrose Street, Belgrave.

Annie died on 28th September 1932, aged 69 years and was buried in Belgrave Cemetery.

Jackson, Gertrude (1898 - 1965)

Gertrude was born on 25th January 1898 at Hunslet, Yorkshire, to Walter and Annie Jackson.

She moved down to Belgrave, Leicester and lived with her parents in Melrose Street. She attended Catherine Street School and left school when she was almost 15.

Not a great deal is known about Gertrude, but she is remembered as a happy lady with a very bubbly character. Gertrude never married and lived in Braunstone until her death on 31st March 1965.

Jackson, Walter (1863 - 1935)

Walter was born on 18th January 1863 in Hunslet, Yorkshire.
He was a carpenter and married Annie Elizabeth Carr, a Woollen Cloth Weaver in Hunslet on Christmas Day 1889.

Sometime between 1901 and 1905, the family of nine moved to Leicester and came to live in Melrose Street, Belgrave.

Over the years Walter's occupation is recorded as Journeyman Carpenter and Cabinet Maker, and also a Perambulator Maker.

Walter died on 14th August 1935 aged 72 years.

Walter with, *(left to right)* wife Annie, Albert, Ada & Lillian

Wood, Ada (1891 - 1967)

Ada Jackson was born on 2nd June 1891 in Hunslet, Yorkshire to Walter and Annie Jackson.

When they moved to Belgrave, Leicester in the early 1900s, she went to Willow Street School, leaving just before her 14th birthday.

Like many girls of her age she then got a job in the hosiery industry and went to A.W. Swann's hosiery firm in Leicester as a Machinist.

She married Horace Raymond Dixey Wood, an Oadby man who worked in the wine and spirit trade, on 5th August 1918 at St. Michael and All Angels Church, Belgrave, Leicester.

After the birth of her children, Ada gave up her job in the hosiery.

During the second World War Ada and Horace took in evacuees and had a mother and her two children living with them.

Living on the Saffron Lane Estate, they had two sons, Raymond and Norman.

Ada died on 31st January 1967 aged 75 years.

Wood, Horace Raymond Dixey (1894 - 1969)

Horace was born on 23rd June 1894 in Oadby, and whilst growing up was a choir boy at St. Peter's Church, Oadby.

After leaving school he initially worked as a clerk in a hosiery firm.

Horace had served in the Great War in the 3rd Leicestershire Regiment, serving as a rifleman in France and Flanders. He was to suffer from gas poisoning which affected his breathing in later life.

He married Ada Jackson on 5th August 1918, at St Michael and All Angel's Church, Belgrave.

After the war he worked in the wine and spirit trade at W. & A. Gilbeys, eventually becoming Manager. He stayed there for the rest of his working life

He and Ada brought up two sons, Raymond and Norman.

Horace's main hobby was golf and he was a member of both Scraptoft and Western Park Golf Clubs. He was also President of the Leicester Artisans.

Horace died on 10th July 1969, aged 75 years.

The grave contains Annie Elizabeth Jackson died 28th September 1932 aged 69 years, her husband Walter Jackson died 14th August 1935 aged 72 years, Gertrude Jackson died 31st March 1965 aged 65 years, sister to Ada.

The grave also contains Ada Wood, Annie and Walter's daughter who died on 31st January 1967 aged 75 years. Horace's ashes are scattered nearby.

Horace Wood & Ada Jackson

Guilford, Charles Thomas (1880 - 1966)

Charles Thomas Guilford was born in July 1880 and was the eldest son of John and Jane Guilford.

Known as Charlie, he went to school at St Margaret's in Grade VI.

He married Florence Ann Moore in May 1913 at St. Mark's Church, Leicester and they had one daughter.

Charles served in the Great War in the RASC, (Royal Army Service Corps).

He played the piano and also had an allotment on Red Hill (near where the petrol station is now).

He died in September 1966 in Hillcrest Nursing Home on Swain Street, Leicester, aged 86 years.

Guilford, Florence Ann (1873 - 1955)

Florence Ann Moore was born in July 1873 and was the daughter of Nodous and Susanna Moore, and sister to Clara, Lily, Ada, Walter and Thomas Moore. *(See Plots D484 & D298)*

She married Charles Thomas Guilford in May 1913 at St Mark's Church, Leicester, and they had one daughter, Marjorie Lilian.

Florence worked in the hosiery at Griswold's as a Hosiery Hand.

Every Tuesday she used to travel by bus from Belgrave to Birstall to see her daughter and family.

She died at 89 Acorn Street on 2nd April 1955 aged 82 years and was laid to rest at Belgrave Cemetery after the funeral service at Harrison Road Methodist Church.

Charles & Florence
Guilford

Guilford, Jane (1858 - 1929)

Jane Foster was born in Leicester in 1858.

She married James Thomas Guilford (known as Thomas) in December 1878 at St Mark's Church, Belgrave.

She had five children, two daughters and three sons although her first child died.

Jane died in 24th July 1929, aged 71 years, at 310 Syston Street, Leicester and was laid to rest on 29th July.

Guilford, John Thomas (1857 - 1932)

John Thomas was born in Derby in May 1857 and was known as Thomas.

His father was a gardener. In the 1861 Census the family were in Bradford. By the time of the next census they had moved to Leicester.

He married Jane Foster in December 1878 at St Mark's Church, Belgrave, and they had five children.

John worked in the shoe trade as a Shoe Finisher, Shoe Clicker, and Shoe maker.

He died on 27th May 1932 aged 76 years, at 310 Syston Street, Leicester and was laid to rest on 31st May 1932 with his wife Jane Guilford, 1929, aged 71 years and his son Charles Thomas, 1966 aged 86 years and Charles's wife Florence, 1955 aged 82 years

Cramp, William Norman (1897 - 1928)

William Norman Cramp was born in 1897 at an address in Belgrave Gate, the grandson of Nodous and Susannah Moore and son of Ada Cramp née Moore and James Cramp.

He saw service and survived World War I, but unfortunately died of throat cancer at 127 Cranbourne Street, Belgrave aged 31 years on 14th June 1928.

He was laid to rest in Belgrave Cemetery on Monday 18th June 1928, his funeral service having taken place at 3pm at Hill Street United Methodist Chapel.

Moore, Nodous (1847 - 1920)

Nodous was born in Burleys Way in 1847.

He married Susannah Ward at St Mary De Castro, Leicester in 1866 and they had 10 children. Unfortunately only four girls survived, Clara, Lily, Ada and Florence. The boys all died young, the eldest before reaching his 31st birthday.

According to the parochial electors, he had freehold land in Orton Road from 1896 to 1907. He was also employed in hosiery work as a Spinning Mills Mechanic.

He died at 34 Olphin Street, which he rented, on 1st July 1920, aged 72 years and was laid to rest on 5th July 1920.

Nodous & Susannah
Moore & Walter?

Moore, Susannah (1846 - 1925)

Susannah Ward was born in 1846 at Great Wigston. She married Nodous Moore in December 1866 at St Mary De Castro, Leicester.

She had ten children, but only the girls survived. Ada, Lily, Florence and Clara lived until well into their 80s and 90s.

Susannah died at 34 Olphin Street on 2nd April 1925, aged 78 years.

Moore, Thomas (1879 - 1911)

Thomas was the son of Nodous and Susannah Moore. Born in July 1879 he went to school at Catherine Street, Belgrave, Leicester in Grade VI.

In 1903 he emigrated to Canada, departing from Liverpool on the ship 'Sicilian',and arriving at Halifax, Nova Scotia on 7th April 1903. He stated in his letter home that he slept six to a bunk and it was a very slow boat.

He travelled to Meaford and ended up at Moosejaw, Canada where he unfortunately died on 22nd March 1911 aged 31 years, of an ulcer of the stomach. He was buried in Moosejaw Cemetery, on 25th March 1911.

Moore, Walter (1889 - 1915)

Walter was a son of Nodous and Susannah Moore, born in July 1889. By the 1911 Census, he is shown as a Cabinet Maker.

He became engaged to Sarah Jane Hill (Ginny), but died before they could be married.

He died at 34 Olphin Street, Belgrave in September 1915 aged 26 years, of appendicitis and was laid to rest on 4th October 1915. With him are his parents, Nodous Moore died 1920 aged 72, Susannah Moore, died 1925 aged 78, and his nephew, William Norman Cramp, died 1928, aged 31. His brother Thomas is also remembered on the memorial stone.

Bromley, Mary Elizabeth (1865 - 1956)

It was a fine sight every Sunday morning when a young man riding his penny farthing bicycle travelled from Holden Street, Belgrave to Nottingham to woo his love. He was on his way to court Mary Elizabeth Fox, always known in the family as Lizzie. His name was Robert Bromley, born on 16th August 1857.

Robert worked as a Silks man, as far as the family can gather, he was the man who refined the flour using a silk mesh, a procedure called 'dressing'. Employed at Thompson's Flour Mill on Soar Lane, Leicester as part of his work he regularly called on Charles Fox, a master baker and flour seller, who had a bakery on Radford Road, Hyson Green, Nottingham. It was there that his eyes first met those of Lizzie. They married on 22nd September 1885 at the General Baptist Chapel, Basford. He was 29, she was 20.

Lizzie was born in Worksop on 21st November 1865 to Charles and Caroline Fox. She had three sisters, Sarah Ann, Alice and Fanny as well as a brother William Henry. During the 1870's the family had moved to Old Basford, Nottingham, where Caroline had been born. They took up residence at 5, Lincoln Terrace on the opposite side of the road to the Mill, where Charles worked. They moved into the bakery on Radford Road, Hyson Green and set up in business in the early 1880s.

Robert & Mary Elizabeth Bromley, son Charles Robert *(left)*
early 1920s

After their wedding, Lizzie and Robert moved into a cottage in Bath Lane, Leicester, near to the Soar Lane Mill. After a few years they moved to Belgrave and lived in Beaumanor Road, moving on to Gypsy Road, Melton Road and eventually Vicarage Lane, Belgrave.

They had four children, Ethel, Charles Robert, Harry born 1892 and Louisa born 19th June 1898. Unfortunately Harry died aged eight months in 1893; so Robert and Lizzie bought the first of the families graves in Belgrave Cemetery at a cost of £1.17s.0d (£1.87½).(Plot D716)

Lizzie busied herself with her remaining children. She also became involved with the Chapel and set up sewing meetings for the local ladies, teaching them sewing, knitting and crochet. This she did at both Claremont Street and Carey Hall. She also taught the Ellis sisters at Belgrave Hall how to crochet. She was a strong non-conformist or 'Nonnie' as they were known. All her life she regularly read her Bible every morning and evening.

The family grave (Plot D716) was again opened when Robert's parents, Robert snr, aged 87 years died in 1909 and Harriet Bromley (née Allen), aged 79 years, died in 1902, and where they now rest with their young grandson Harry.

Robert snr and Harriet had both been born in Suffolk and moved to Belgrave in the 1870's with their young family, Louisa, Robert jnr, Frances and George. Robert snr was a farmer who fattened bullocks on land near Thurmaston and Barkby.

Lizzie's son Charles Robert married Lina Loretta Sidwell and they had one son, Kenneth. Sadly he was shot accidentally at his RAF passing out parade in 1942 by a sten gun, which should not have been loaded. This was a terrible shock to all the family.

Ethel married Reginald Tite who was a Manager at the British United Shoe Machinery Company.

Louisa Bromley
aged 24 - 1922

Robert was buried in the second family grave (Plot D714) at Belgrave, near to his son and parents after his death on 15th April 1922, aged 65 years. The plot was purchased for the family by Ethel at a cost of £3.14s.0d (£3.70).

Louisa married Louis Wilfred Gladstone Newick at St. Peter's Church, Belgrave in 1923, just one year after her father had passed away. Louis worked for the Hoover Company before becoming a Manager at Morgan Squire's store in Market Street.

Robert's sister Louisa, born in 1856, after whom he had named his daughter, is also in the Cemetery, (Plot B638). She had married William Holland, who was a Butcher with a shop in Loughborough Road. He died in 1915 and she joined him in 1927 aged 71 years. They are laid to rest with Lilian Maud Chamberlin née Holland born 1880, died October 1968 aged 88 years and Edgar Lionel Chamberlin, born 1871, died March 1968 aged 97 years (William and Louisa's daughter and son-in-law). All were residing at the family home at 3 Elmdale Street at the time of their deaths.

The outbreak of the Second World War found Lizzie living in the Western Park area with her daughter Louisa, son-in-law Louis Newick born 3rd July 1895 and their children Geoffrey and Kathleen.

Lizzie carried on her good works by knitting socks for the Armed Forces. She received a letter of thanks from Mrs Churchill for her efforts in knitting white socks, gloves and balaclavas for her Aid to Russia Fund. These helped Russian soldiers keep warm and camouflaged during their dreadful snowy winters.

The family still have examples of her needlework including lace trimmed night gowns, which were worn by all the grandchildren. Lizzie Bromley was always there with a helping hand for anybody. She was truly loved by all her family and friends and is still sadly missed.

Maidstone & District Charabanc, Tenterden, Kent – 1922
left to right: Edith Tite, Louisa Newick, Lina Bromley

At the age of 91, after having outlived Robert by thirty four years, Lizzie joined him at Belgrave Cemetery on 9th October 1956, followed by their daughter, Louisa Newick née Bromley, in 1983 aged 84 years, her husband Louis Newick in 1986, aged 90 years and the ashes of their son Geoffrey Newick, born 14th April 1924, on 3rd July 2007 aged 83 years, although there is no mention of him on the memorial inscription he will be added shortly.

Ross, Joseph (1838 - 1906)

Joseph was born on 14th November 1838. He was married twice, firstly to Frances Halford on the 15th December 1856 at St Margaret's Church, Leicester. They had nine children.

Frances died on 10th February 1891. Joseph married again on 31st December 1891 at St Matthew's Church, Leicester and his second wife, Caroline Rose gave him four more children.

Joseph was a Shoemaker by trade and lived in Leicester all his life.

He died on 14th October 1906 at 33, Acorn Street, Leicester, aged 68 years. He is buried with his sister, Eliza Groocock née Ross, who died in October 1912 aged 82 years, and his son John Rose Ross who died in July 1901 aged two and a half years, also at 33 Acorn Street, Belgrave, Leicester.

Fantham, Cissy May (1903 - 1995)

Cissy May White was born on 27th January 1903, fourth child of George and Clara White. She attended the small school on Dover Street, which is now a chapel, and then she moved on to Narborough Road School presumably when the family moved to Norman Street. From the few family photos of the children held by the family, she always seemed to have a stern or cross look on her face.

Cissy left school at fourteen, the family still have her Certificate of Education and permission to leave school in 1916 and it shows she could read and write.

She too went to work at W. Burtons Spinners and Dyers as did her sisters Ida and Grace, but by her own admission, she was not very good and was put into the office as a junior where she stayed for the next fifty years.

Her social life revolved around the same pursuits as her siblings, but it was at work where she met her future husband George Fantham, who was a van driver there.

Cissy was a good looking girl and on 31st March 1928 at the Church of the Martyrs, Westcotes Drive, she and George were married.

They went to live at 80 Lambert Road, Leicester.

It is interesting to note that Cissy put down the deposit on the house and took out the mortgage as a single female which was an unusual event at that time. The house cost £425.

The newly married couple certainly lived their lives to the full as the family have a photograph of Cissy and George's Uncle Arthur in a bi-plane after a flight.

However, after a very short marriage, George died of a heart attack on 29th April 1932 at the age of twenty eight.

Cissy was devastated and she was to mourn him for the rest of her life. She purchased a grave in Belgrave Cemetery and the gravestone reflected Cissy's love for George,

"God gives us love,
Someone to Love he only Lends".

Cissy now devoted herself to her work and became secretary to the directors of W. Burton and Sons. She could take shorthand at a fantastic speed and dealt with the company customers in a very professional manner.

She took holidays to visit friends and relations and got quite adventurous when she went to Norway.

She retired in 1966 after 50 years at W. Burtons. It is interesting to note that her sister Ida was still working there aged sixty-eight.

Although retired, Cissy was still very sprightly; she visited George's grave every week at Belgrave to keep it tidy, she looked after Ida when her health started to fail, and when walking with Cissy, the family had to run to keep up!

Later on the family took her with them on holiday, visiting the Scilly Isles one year where Cissy broke her ankle, but she didn't let it spoil anyone's holiday. Once in plaster she coped well with everything, including the journey home on the train back to Derby!

After Bill, Cissy's brother-in-law, died, she and her sister Grace grew closer together again. There were regular holidays together with the family and the vision of the two sisters sitting together on the sea front at Sheringham, complete with headscarves and big coats on chatting away about the good old days is a lasting happy family memory.

Cissy eventually became ill and after a major operation she made a recovery, but by then the cancer had spread and she died in LOROS Hospice on 15th April 1995.

Cissy's funeral took place at the Church of the Martyrs where she had been married and she was finally reunited with George and laid to rest at Belgrave Cemetery.

Radford, Grace Alexandria (1900 - 1998)

Grace Alexandria White was born on 17th July 1900, third child to Edward and Clara White, 1 Court, Chatham Street, Leicester.

At this point a slight digression: Grace's uncle George (her father's brother) was well known as 'Sticky' White, one of the three leaders of the March of the Unemployed Men from Leicester to London in 1905. A cripple from birth and despite walking with a stick, he was the only one of the leaders who walked all the way to London and back with the unemployed men. *(An excellent account of the march is available from the Record Office and well worth reading! Ed.)*

Grace was the second of three daughters, Ida Anne born in 1898 and Cissy May born in 1903 also an older son, George Edward, born in 1896. They attended the small school in Dover Street, Leicester.

By the time that she left school aged 14, in 1914, the family had moved to 70 Norman Street and Grace and her elder sister Ida were employed at W. Burton and Sons, Western Road, yarn spinners and dyers.

Grace worked on the shop floor as a Yarn Spinner. The hours were long and the working week of 50 hours was very poorly paid.

During her teens she met William Arthur Radford and they started courting, marrying on 5th August 1922 at the Church of the Martyrs, Westcotes Drive, Leicester. After they were married they rented rooms at 348 Western Road, Leicester.

Their first child Kenneth William Radford was born on 24th July 1925 at Westcotes Maternity Home.

As the family had grown, it would appear that they moved out of number 348, first into a council house and a short time later into 78 Norman Street, close to Grace's mum and dad at number 70.

Grace carried on working at Burton's in the winding room.

Grace in the Winding Room

On 26th April 1934, Grace and Bill's second son, Keith, was born at home. When the two children were small, they were child-minded and Grace returned to work at Burtons.

Grace's nickname at Burtons was 'Tom' because of her ginger hair.

Just after the outbreak of war, a bomb fell in a street near to W. Burtons and blew the doors off the factory yard.

A short time after this Kathleen was born on the 13th December 1941 and Bill joined the Home Guard.

Grace and Bill's son Ken joined the Royal Marines, seeing active service and eventually he went to France on D-Day, fortunately coming back unscathed.

Just before the war ended Trevor was born on 10th January 1944.

In the 1950's, Grace and Bill bought number 78 Norman Street for approximately £500 after renting it for so many years. Bill left his driving job and went to work at the British United Shoe Machinery Co. as a Maintenance Engineer. Grace was still at Burtons.

After 50 years, Grace finally retired in 1964. She was presented with a clock, but even after all those years of loyalty she wasn't entitled to a pension.

Instead of taking life easy, Grace started to look after elderly neighbours. She also looked after her sister Ida when she became too frail to look after herself.

On top of this, there was a gathering of the family complete with children every Saturday, usually with a full roast dinner, served in two sittings round the small dining table.

After their Golden Wedding in 1972, Bill started to suffer with Parkinson's disease and had strokes and heart attacks. Grace continued to look after him, Ida and other elderly neighbours.

Bill died a year after their Diamond Wedding anniversary in 1982.

Ida had died in 1973 and although Grace was now eighty six, she still carried on caring for folk and looking after her younger sister Cissy.

After an accident in 1990, Grace was found in the bathroom with two broken knees. After operations on both knees she made a full recovery at the age of ninety!

Cissy died in 1992 and so now Grace had lost all her sisters and friends.

She continued to be mentally alert and put her good health down to butter, lard, salt and all things that are supposed to be bad for you.

In April 1998 she developed a chest infection and died on April 23rd in her beloved little home.

Grace's ashes are interred in Cissy and George Fantham's grave at Belgrave Cemetery, where a small brass plaque was added to their headstone by the family.

Green, William (1835 - 1900)

William Green was born in 1835, the son of John Jackson Green and Mary Ann née Johnson. The family lived in the old Wharf Street area of the city.

We know from the census returns that he was a Needle Maker as was his brother John Green born in 1844.

The brothers worked for a man by the name of John Wright Smith who left both brothers quite a large sum of money each. Written into his will was "faithful workmen under me in my business".

The family can only think that the brothers took over the business on John Wright Smith's death.

William married Maria Hurst on 25ᵗʰ December 1853 at St. Margaret's Church. Maria had been born in Godalming, Surrey in approximately 1834.

By the 1881 Census they have a total of ten children, eight of whom reached adulthood, Elizabeth, Hannah and Rebecca listed in the 1881 Census as needle makers along with their father, son Alfred working as a smith in an iron foundry and another son as a hosiery warehouseman. Two other children, Alfred and William were still at school at this time and they were all living at 287 Belgrave Road, Leicester. It would appear that Maria was a hard working wife and mother to this large family.

Only two of their daughters married, Elizabeth to John Dexter, and Hannah to George Ross, Rebecca remaining single.

William and Maria are great, great grandparents and Hannah great grandmother to the contributor.

Hannah died before her parents so no family photos were passed down to this side of the family.

William died on 17ᵗʰ April 1900, aged 64. on the stone was written; *"For thou art my refuge and my fortress, In thee have I put my trust"*.

Maria his wife, died not long after on 17ᵗʰ December 1901, aged 66 years. Her inscription reads; *"Say not Goodnight - but in some brighter clime, Bid us Good morning"*.

William and Maria were living at 43 Melton Road, Belgrave at the time of their deaths.

They are both laid to rest with their youngest son, Arthur, who died in July 1970 aged 98 years and his wife Adeline, who died March 1953 aged 79 years. They were both resident at East Park Road, Leicester at that time.

The picture shows the memorial headstone of this family as it is of particular interest, being a beautifully-made anchor and chain enclosing a cross. Mounted on three steps, denoting faith, hope and charity, the anchor itself also denotes hope. Also on this late Victorian stone are biblical and hymn verses so very typical of the time.

📖

Middleton, Ann (1873 - 1938)

Ann Shipley was born on 11th August 1873 at 52 Crab Street, Leicester and was one of eleven children born to Joseph and Mary Ann Shipley.
Ann married Arthur Thomas Middleton on 10th June 1898 at St Mary de Castro in Leicester. They had ten children, eight of whom survived into adulthood.
Ann died on 30th May 1938 from heart failure, aged 65 years.

Arthur & Ann Middleton

Middleton, Arthur Thomas (1873 - 1957)

Arthur Thomas was born in Holme, Huntingdonshire on 29th June 1873.
On 10th June 1898, he married Ann Shipley at Mary de Castro Church in Leicester.
They lived at 59 Beaumanor Road, Belgrave and had ten children.
Arthur was employed by the Leicester City Corporation as a Head Gardener and liked nothing better than to maintain the bowling green at Abbey Park where he was a member for many years.
Together with his bowls partner Arthur Ward he won the England Pairs Dewar Cup in 1925. As can be seen from the photograph, they were a very successful pair.
Later in his life Arthur was employed as a Shoe Warehouseman.
He died from a cerebral thrombosis on 17th February 1957 aged 84 years and was laid to rest with Ann, his wife who died on 30th May 1938 aged 65 years. At the time of their deaths they were still living at Beaumanor Road.

Arthur Middleton *(right)* & bowls partner Arthur Ward

Clayton, Edwin (1872 - 1931)

Edwin was born in 1872 in Belgrave, Leicester, son to Edwin and Eliza Clayton, his father being at the time of the 1881 Census a framework knitter.

Edwin jnr. had three siblings at this time, Elizabeth, born 1870, William, born 1876, and Samuel born 1879. The family were living at 60 Checketts Road, Belgrave.

By 1891, the census records that the family have moved to 43 Checketts Road and Edwin, now aged 19 is a Shoe Clicker. His sister is a Shoe Fitter and William is an Agricultural Labourer.

In 1901 there is only a completed census form for Edwin and his father, the address being 2 Little Avenue, Belgrave. Edwin snr is now a Stone Mason's Labourer and still married, and Edwin jnr is a Coal Dealer. There is no sign of wife or other children on the form.

Other than the paper work we can find, the family are aware that he was employed at various times as a journeyman, coach painter and house painter.

Edwin married Hannah Rivers at Burton-on-Trent in the summer of 1907 and they eventually moved to Leicester having first lived in Coventry when newly married and where the family was living during the 1911 Census.

Edwin died aged 60 in November 1931.

Clayton, Hannah (1874 - 1952)

Hannah Rivers was born on 20th August 1874 to George and Evelina Rivers at Stapenhill near Burton-on-Trent.

Although 26 years old, on the 1901 Census, Hannah is still living with her parents at 19 Brizlincote Street, Stapenhill, Derbyshire and she is employed as a 'Housekeeper Domestic'. Whether as a help to her family or elsewhere isn't known.

She married Edwin Clayton in the summer of 1907 at Burton-on-Trent and eventually moved to Leicester having first lived in Coventry when newly married and where the family was living during the 1911 Census. This shows that her only daughter, Elizabeth May, is three years old and they are living at 88 Coronation Road, Coventry.

The family then moved to Leicester at sometime and took up residence at 2 Little Avenue, Belgrave, where Elizabeth May, was to grow up.

Hannah's husband, Edwin, died in November 1931, a few months after Elizabeth married on 30th May 1931.

It is remembered by Hannah's grand-daughter that Grandma Hannah always "spoilt me to death".

Hannah carried on living in Little Avenue until the house got too much for her to cope with and she later moved into Loughborough Road Cottages, Loughborough Road, Belgrave which were situated opposite the allotments, where she was to continue to live until she died. Hannah died in November 1952 aged 78 years.

Robinson, Elizabeth May (1908 - 1995)

Elizabeth May Clayton was born in 1908, and was always known as Betty. Her parents were Edwin and Hannah Clayton who lived at 2 Little Avenue, off Checketts Road, Belgrave where Elizabeth lived until she married Harry Edwin Robinson at St Michael and All Angel's Church on 30th May 1931 when she was 23. Then they started their married life on the Sutton Estate and later moved into Checketts Close after it was newly built.

Elizabeth worked at Greenlees Ltd in Doncaster Road, Belgrave, a well known boot and shoe company. Her job was to put the sock linings inside the shoes.

She loved making herself look nice, getting dressed up and going out with Harry. She loved travelling the world with her husband and both loved life. So they were really made for each other.

Her daughter remembers her as a loving mother who always had time for her and to have a cuddle on her lap and a kiss.

When Elizabeth died on 18th April 1995 aged 86 years, she was resident at 'Elmlands', Stoneygate Road, Leicester.

Elizabeth & Harry Edwin on their wedding day, 1931

93

Robinson, Harry Edwin (1902 - 1975)

Harry Edwin Robinson was born in Moira, Leicestershire on 30th August 1902 to Albert and Alice Maud Robinson.

He had five sisters, Ada, Hilda Maud, Jessie Maria, Edith May, Lilian Alice and five brothers, Albert Edwin, Arthur Albert Victor, James William, Leslie Robert George, one of whom is remembered on the war memorial in Town Hall Square, Leicester.

The family lived in Lancashire Street, Belgrave and whilst growing up Harry attended Harrison Road School.

He worked at the B.U. (British United Shoe Machinery Company) as a clerk for 30 or 40 years.

He married Elizabeth May Clayton at St Michael and All Angels Church on Melton Road, Belgrave, on 30th May 1931.

They both loved to travel and Harry and Betty as Elizabeth preferred to be called, travelled all over the world until their daughter was born.

He was always considered a nice man by his family.

Harry Edwin died on 22nd August 1975 aged 77 years and was living at 32 Checketts Close at the time he died. and is laid to rest with his wife, Elizabeth May in Belgrave Cemetery. She died on 18th April 1975 aged 86, whilst living at Elmlands, Stoneygate, Leicester.

Also buried with them are Harry's father-in-law, Edwin Clayton, who died November 1931 aged 60 years, and mother-in-law Hannah Clayton, who died November 1952 aged 86 years.

Wolfe, George (1909 - 1979)

George was born in Dunbar Road, Belgrave on 20th April 1909, to George Henry Wolfe and Elizabeth Jane Wolfe née Bedford and on leaving Ellis Avenue School (he apparently spoke excellent French) he became an Engineer Pattern Maker.

He married Lily Hamplett, (known as Connie). She was born in December 1910 in Colton Street, north east Leicester.

Connie worked as a catering supervisor at Woolworth's restaurant, Gallowtree Gate and was always known as Miss Hamplett, even after her marriage to George. Connie was an Air Raid warden working from the top of Woolworth's during the Second World War catering for the Forces and the public.

After the birth of her two children she changed her employment to Hosiery Machinist/ Embroiderer.

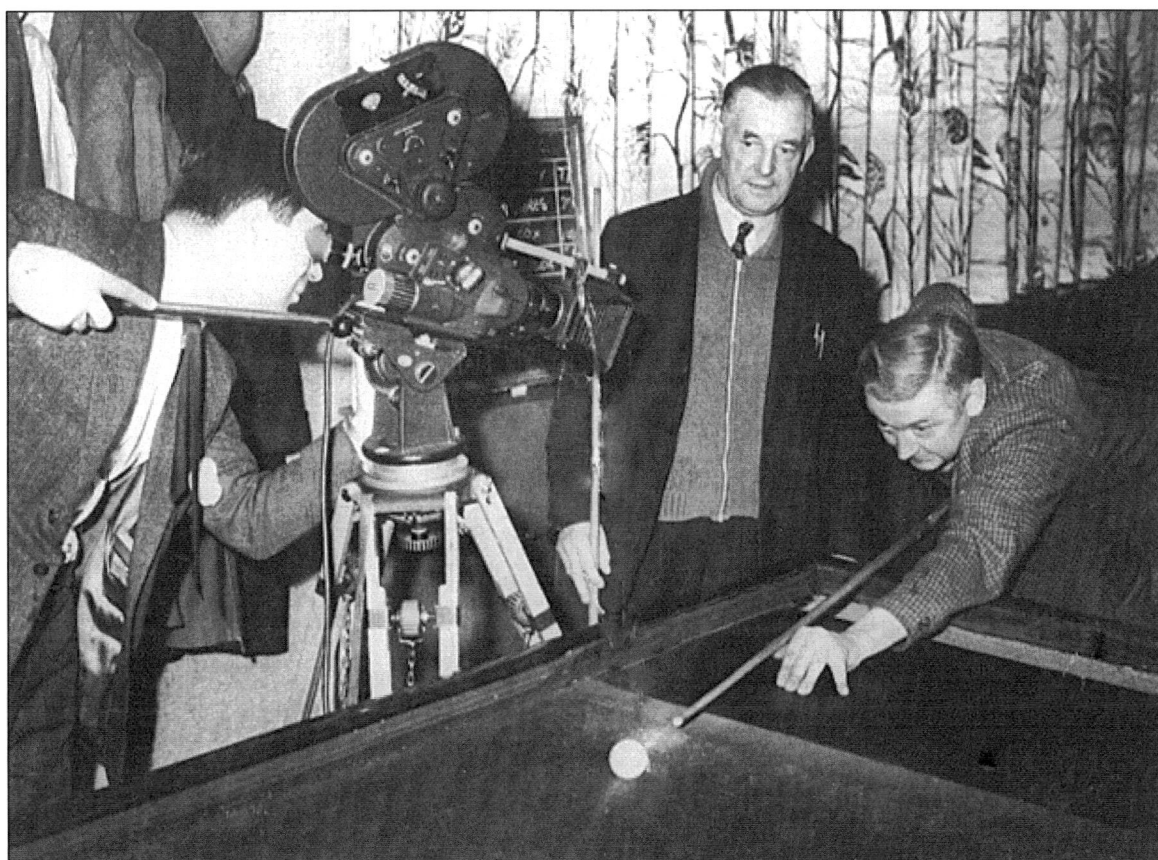

George applied to join the Navy in 1939 at the outbreak of war but he was turned down as he was in a reserved occupation.

George was an excellent billiards player and won many trophies. A photograph is included showing him with his billiard cue, playing at the Belgrave Liberal Club, during an interview which was also being televised for BBC Grandstand in 1955/56.

The family could not see the television interview as they had no television at that time, neither have they any photographs of George's Mum and Dad as they both died when George was just a teenager.

The Wolfe/Wilson/Hamplett/Bedford families have all lived in Vann Street at various addresses in the early years. *(See George Henry Wolfe Plot D1035)*

George Wolfe died on 2nd May 1979 aged 70 years.

Wolfe, George Henry (1881 - 1922)

George Henry was born in Leire Street, Belgrave in January 1881 and after leaving school he became a Fruit Merchant's Drayman.

By the 1891 Census, Elizabeth Jane née Bedford and her family were living at 33 Vann Street, Belgrave, not far from the home of George Henry, and in Autumn 1907 he married Elizabeth, who was born in Hinckley in 1882. She was a hosiery machinist.

In the 1911 Census the family were living at 62 Twycross Street, Leicester, a shop with five rooms where George was operating as a green-grocer dealer and Elizabeth was helping in the business.

By this time they had one child, named after his father, George, aged one year.

George Henry fought in the Great War joining the British Army, Royal Field Artillery and was awarded the Victory Medal.

He died on 24th October 1922 at the young age of 41 years. Such was the great esteem in which George Henry was held by his colleagues, his memorial stone was erected by the Wholesale and Retail Fruiterers to show their high regard. His wife and family must have been very proud.

George Henry was buried in Belgrave Cemetery, to be followed by Elizabeth Jane, his wife when she died on 5th September 1928 aged 46 and later George his son was reunited with them on 2nd May 1979, aged 70 years.

Lily (Connie) died in February 1994. Her father Charles (Chas) Hamplett died when she was two years old in 1913. Rose Hamplett (née Wilson) died 1963. They have a family grave at Gilroes Cemetery Leicester.

Godsall, Gladys Beatrice (1904 - 1993)

Gladys Beatrice was born on 22nd October 1904 to William and May Louisa Godsall at Aston, Warwickshire. She was one of eight children and was always known as Glad, such was her nature, always laughing.

She suffered all her life with deafness and was so self-conscious about this affliction that she never married.

Living most of her life with her family at 73 Flax Road, Belgrave, she looked after her father, William, after her mother died and then nursed her older brother Bill until his death, in 1970.

She worked as a Wool Spinner at Bastard's Wool Spinners on Frog Island, Leicester and later at Wykes Spinners in Barkby Road, Leicester.

Gladys was a member of the choir at Carey Hall, Catherine Street, as were several of her sisters and she had a strong melodious voice, a talent which ran through the family, making Christmas and family parties very joyous, hilarious and so very memorable.

Glad looked after anyone who lived in her street who was in difficulties, a trait that she inherited from her mother May and the family remember seeing her plate up an extra meal for someone who was ill or a widowed husband struggling to hold down his job, and run across the road to her neighbours with the meal covered by a tea towel to keep it warm.

Family remembrances of Glad were of her lovely smiling face and jolly laugh.

Gladys died on 16th January 1993 aged 88 years.

Godsall, May Louisa (1878 - 1939)

May Louisa Dugmore was born in Birmingham, Warwickshire in 1878, one of two children. Her brother became 1st mate on HMS Warspite. (This ship won battle honours in both the Great War and later in World War II.)

Little is known of May's early life, but she nursed her mother until she died aged 54 years.

She married William Godsall in the early part of 1899, and their marriage certificate shows she was employed as a French Polisher at that time.

May Louisa with her young baby

She soon gave birth to Rose, born in Birmingham in 1900 swiftly followed by her first son, William jnr. (known as Bill), born in Tipton, Staffordshire in 1901. She was to have another seven children in the years before moving to 73 Flax Road, Belgrave, Leicester; Edith, (1901) Daisy Winifred, (1903) Gladys Beatrice, (1904) John Ernest, (known as Jack) (1906) and Doris Irene, (known in the family as Don) (1908) who was born in Leicester as was Cyril who was born between July and September 1911, and Frederick in March 1914.

May was forced to cope with tragedy when her son Cyril, aged only seven, was killed by a runaway horse and cart at the bottom of Flax Road, where the family lived. Luckily, unlike Cyril, Fred, who was with him, managed to jump out of the way of the wheels of the cart although he was kicked by the horse and received injuries but survived the ordeal.

May had a hard life with a big family, but it would appear that she was a kind but feisty lady. On one occasion when her eldest son, a gentle and quiet lad, came home from school with his hands in shreds from the cane. May went to the school, demanding to see the teacher. The headmaster asked why and she told him she was about to give him some punishment like he had handed out to her son. By all accounts the teacher was chased around the building by May, with the teacher shouting 'Get this mad woman off me!' It must have been quite a sight, but her son didn't get ill-treated again!

She died just at the beginning of the Second World War on 28th October 1939 aged 61 years so fortunately didn't have to suffer the loss of her youngest son Frederick in June 1944 at Caen in France.

When May Louisa's grave memorial was installed, the gentleman who provided the green chippings for the decorative infill on top of the grave, went to see her family and explained that he would be completing the work free of charge. When asked why he explained that in his childhood, his family also lived in Flax Road and were very poor. He said that if it hadn't been for the kindness of May in providing dinners for them and other kindnesses, his family would have starved and it was his way of showing his family's respect and gratitude to her.

Godsall, William (1877 - 1955)

William Godsall was born in 1877 in Tipton, Stafffordshire, to William and Sarah Godsall, and was one of twelve children.

He left school at 13 and went to work on a farm in Herefordshire where he was treated badly and was whipped when things went wrong.

He married May Louisa Dugmore, early in 1899, in Aston, Warwickshire. She was a French polisher from Birmingham.

By 1901 when he was 24, he had moved to Birmingham with his family and they soon had two children, Rose aged one and a young baby, William jnr. They were living at 50 Wolesley Street, Aston.

William was employed as a Screw Cutter according to the 1901 Census, and somewhere around this time he went to night school to study engineering.

Hard work and an aptitude for engineering allowed him to get on well and so by 1911 the family were living at 73 Flax Road, Belgrave, Leicester and William's occupation is declared on the census as Iron Turner General Engineering. He had begun work at Russell's foundry in Bath Lane.

The family now included Edith, (1901) Daisy Winifred, (1903) Gladys Beatrice, (1904) John Ernest, (known as Jack) (1906) and Doris Irene, (known in the family as Don) (1908). Cyril was born between July and September 1911. We hear no more of Rose in the census.

By the 1930s William was skilled enough to make the flywheel for the Queen Mary and went to Glasgow to see it installed in the ship. He was very clever and although he retired when in his 70's, Russell's Foundry, his old employer, would fetch him back to the factory when a job needed special skills.

William is remembered as a kindly man who always dressed very smartly and his grand daughter remembers that he always wore a flower in his buttonhole every day.

William died on 18th July 1955 aged 80 years, and is resting with his wife, May Louisa Godsall, who died on 28th October 1939 aged 61 years, and his daughter Gladys Beatrice Godsall who died 16th January 1993 aged 88 years.

William and May were both still living at the family home in Flax Road, Belgrave on the dates of their deaths. Gladys died at Courtview Nursing Home, New Walk, Leicester.

Savage, Esther (1866 - 1923)

Savage, William (1866 - 1924)

William Savage was born in 1866 and was the second son of John and Marie Savage who at the time of the 1881 Census lived at 1 Milton Street in the Parish of St. Margaret's. Both John and William are listed as Framework Knitters

In 1885 William married Esther Booth of Sheppey, Kent, at Billesdon. The reason behind Esther's move from Kent to Leicestershire is unfortunately unknown, as is much of her life story. However, we do know that her first daughter Rachel was born in 1885 (could this have been a shotgun wedding?).

There is no trace on the 1891 Census of the family but by the time of the 1901 Census William and Esther were living at 28 Foundry Lane, in the Parish of St. Marks, Leicester with eight children in six rooms! William's occupation was now a Hosiery Hand.

By the time of 1911 Census, William and Esther have moved to 6 Foundry Square, just round the corner in the Parish of St Mark's, indeed not far from the church itself.

They were now coping with nine children in seven rooms. (The two eldest children listed in the 1901 Census were not included in 1911). William's occupation was once again described as "framework knitter – men's jersey" (almost certainly employed at Corah's just up the road from his new home).

The 1911 Census also confirms that William and Esther had a total of thirteen children of which two had died by that time. The thirteenth and final child was Clifford Savage, our contributor's father, who was born in 1910.

Of the eleven known children five were male and six female:

Rachel, the first born in 1885, Arthur born in 1886 is thought to have served in the Royal Navy in World War I.

Next came Georgina who was born in 1888 and was still alive in the 1940s. Winifred was born in 1890 but was never mentioned in the family.

Nellie was born in 1892 and married Alfred Emery.

John William was born in 1894, James born in 1899 went on to become a well known local singer being involved in local male voice choirs.

Albert was born in 1901 and Florrie in 1903 became a war bride, marrying a Canadian soldier and emigrating to Canada.

Lily came next in 1905 and Clifford in 1910 surviving until just short of his 94th birthday and dying in 2004. Rachel, Nellie, John William, James, Albert, Florrie, Lily and Clifford all lived until at least 1952 if not longer, but most of the dates are unknown.

This family probably qualifies as one of the largest surviving Belgrave families at that time. Nine of them were alive in the 1950s and known to our contributor when he was a teenager.

Most of his uncles and aunts worked in the hosiery and knitwear trades in Leicester. When talking about their parents it was clear that 'Mother' was very much a 'larger than life' person who 'wore the trousers' and ruled the household with a rod of iron, whilst 'Father' was a very much lower profile parent who tended to disappear 'down the allotment' with his youngest son, Clifford, given the opportunity!

During World War I the family moved to a four story terraced house, 44 Melton Road, (Drayton Terrace), Belgrave and during the war gave lodgings to one or more policemen.

William and Esther who were still living at the Melton Road address died within six months of each other, Esther on 1st December 1923, aged 57 years and William on 6th June 1924, aged 58 years and were laid to rest in Belgrave Cemetery. Alfred Emery, their daughter Nellie's husband, who died in 1977, is also interred in the same grave.

William & Esther at the allotment,
possibly with daughter Rachel

Brown, Susan (1854 - 1932)

Susan Elliott was born in 1854 and descended from the Belgrave families of Elliott, Agar, Horner and Garner.

She married Thomas Brown and they had 18 children, Elizabeth, 1876 (married Pymm), Robert 1879 - 1882 (buried at Welford Road cemetery), Arthur 1880, Emma 1883 - 1918 (married Green, buried in Welford Road) William 1885, Edith 1889 (married Jeeves), George 1891, Ernest 1893 - 1960(?) Susan 1895 - 1975 (married Vines), all of these probably not buried in Belgrave Cemetery.

Several children died in early infancy, Harry, at one year old, at Elmdale Street, Eva at three years old, at Evans Street. Two others died at 20 years of age, Florence Susan and Frederick, at Elmdale Street. They are all buried together at Belgrave. *(see Plot B340)*

After Thomas' death in 1917, Susan lived at 20 Mill Hill, Belgrave.

When she died in December 1932 Susan was aged 78.

Brown, Thomas (1852 - 1917)

Thomas was born in 1852 to Robert and Mary Brown née East.

He lived at various times at Elmdale Street, Evans Street, Cranbourne Street and Newington Street most of which are or were situated in the old Belgrave area of Leicester.

Thomas married Susan née Elliott and they had 18 children. *(Please see known list of children under Susan Brown)*

Thomas died in March 1917, aged 65 years.

Brown, Thomas Charles (1875 - 1923)

Thomas Charles was the eldest son of Thomas and Susan Brown

Born in 1875, little is known about him except that he was soldier for a while and was sent to India. He suffered from malaria.

He was living at 11 The Conery, off Loughborough Road when he died in September 1923, aged 48 years.

He was laid to rest with his father Thomas, who died in March 1917, aged 65 years and his mother Susan, who died December 1932, aged 78 years, in Belgrave Cemetery.

Kingston, Tom (1888? – 1943)

Tom Kingston was from Peterborough, and it is not certain when he moved to Leicester, nor when he took up residence at 16 Royal Road, Belgrave.

He was a Potato Merchant, and during the Great War he was a Cavalry Officer (similar to the book 'War Horse')

He married Ada Page, a nurse, in 1914, in Leicester. She lived in Belgrave and they had four children, Joan, Jack, Peggy and Vera all born at 16 Royal Road.

The family moved to Berridge Lane, Belgrave in approx 1923, to a small holding where Tom was a fruit and vegetable merchant

Tom died in March 1943 aged approx. 61 years and is laid to rest with Ada who joined him in February 1967 aged 85 years. The grave also contains their son and daughter, Jack Kingston who died in August 1981 aged 60 years and Joan Kingston who died in December 1920 aged 8 months. The ashes of Peggy's husband and Tom and Ada's son-in-law Walter Marston, who died on 11th December 1975 aged 59 years are also in the grave.

Vera Kingston died in 1996 and is buried with her husband at Gilroes.

Peggy Kingston died in 2010 aged 95 and was cremated, her ashes and those of her dogs are scattered over fields as was her wish.

📖

Keable, Ernest (1886 - 1969)

Ernest was born in Denton, Norfolk in 1886, and moved to Leicester aged fourteen. He worked on the railways and married Ethel Fretsom, a shoe machinist, on 4th September 1909 at Leicester Registry Office.

They lived at 69 Acorn Street, Belgrave and had a daughter May Ivy, who died in infancy, aged five months and two sons, Ernest jnr. who died in 1972 and Frederick, now aged 83 and still living in Market Harborough.

Frederick was shocked when the Belgrave Cemetery records showed his sister's resting place as he was unaware of her existence until family history searches revealed that she is buried with her parents.

Ernest's son Frederick and his family moved into 69 Acorn Street with Ernest in 1950 after their marriage when there was still no electricity or a bathroom so life must have been tough! Ernest passed away on 17th February 1969.

Keable, Ethel (1885 - 1949)

Ethel Fretsom was born in 1885 at Leicester.

She married Ernest Keable on 4th September 1909 at Leicester Registry Office. The photograph shows Ethel and Ernest on the right of the picture on their wedding day. The other couple are her sister Mabel who was a witness at the wedding, along with Elijah Lingard who was to be Mabel's future husband.

Ethel had quite a few siblings, about seven, plus a set of twins. Her mother had died young in 1907 and at the time of her marriage Ethel was employed as a shoe machinist, and was living at 10 Tudor Road, Leicester. (The house is no longer there, although Tudor Road is. It is not known why, but quite a few were unfit for habitation.)

It is thought that Ethel may have given birth to twins in 1910 but this has yet to be verified. She did have three children, May Ivy, who died in infancy, aged five months in 1921, Ernest who died in 1972 and Frederick who is 83 and still lives at Market Harborough, Leicestershire.

Ernest and Ethel led a very quiet life and

never had much but as can be seen from the later photograph she is obviously in all her finery and looks very affluent.

Ethel died aged 64 years, on 17th April 1949, and it was rumoured that she had died of a broken heart as she was missing her son Frederick who was serving in the army. But in actual fact she had tuberculosis. The loss of May Ivy so young must have contributed to her poor health too.

Ethel is laid to rest at Belgrave Cemetery with Ernest her husband who died in February 1969 aged 83 years and May Ivy her baby daughter.

Ethel & Ernest *(right)* on their wedding day with her sister
Mabel *(left)* and Elijah Lingard
1909

Hatfield, Gweneth Mabel (1914 - 1921)

Daughter of Oliver and Kate Hatfield, Gweneth Mabel was born at 66 Moira Street, Belgrave on 16th August 1914 and christened at St Michael and All Angel's Church, Melton Road, Leicester.

Whilst still a young child, she contracted meningitis, suffering several days with convulsions and the last words she spoke to her father, who was by her bedside, was, 'Look at that bright light, daddy'. She died in the children's wing of the Leicester Royal Infirmary, on 27th May 1921, aged six years.

Her funeral was held at Belgrave Hall Methodist Church, Belgrave Road and school children lined the pavement from the hearse to the church doors.

As her parents had moved to nearby Wand Street, they found that they were no longer able to purchase a burial plot in Belgrave Cemetery. Therefore, her uncle, who lived in Halkin Street, Belgrave where residents could be interred at Belgrave Cemetery, bought the grave plot.

Hatfield, John William (1921 - 1984)

John William was born on 17th March 1921 at 43 Wand Street, Belgrave and christened at St Michael and All Angels Church on 10th July 1921. He moved with his family to 82 Myrtle Road, Highfields in 1926.

John worked for William Gimson and Sons Ltd, Timber Importers, Welford Road and later, Upperton Road from 1935 until his death in 1984. He started as an office boy and rose up to be a director and company secretary and also had a seat on the Board.

He joined the R.A.F. during World War II in 1940 and was sent to Egypt until his demob in 1946.

During his career at Gimsons he travelled extensively throughout Europe, Scandinavia and Canada.

He married Margaret Taylor in 1942 but she died in childbirth in 1947 along with their son John Gaven Hatfield. They were both placed in the same coffin and taken to Scotland for burial. Margaret's mother was a Fleming from north of the border and a cousin of Sir Alexander Fleming, who discovered penicillin.

In 1949 John William was married again, to Esme Helen Jones and they initially lived at 84 Myrtle Road, Highfields in Leicester before moving to a newly built property, 34 Wintersdale Road, near Thurnby, Leicester in 1953.

He was the father of two sons, Glyn and Neil.

John William died of skin cancer on 8th May 1984 at the same age as his father, 63 years, in the Leicester Royal Infirmary.

Sadly his wife Esme couldn't be buried with him when she died in 2007 as the grave plot was now full. Therefore, she was laid to rest next to her sister and brother-in-law in Great Bowden cemetery near Market Harborough, Leicestershire.

Hatfield, Kate (1891 - 1977)

Kate Brown, daughter of William Alfred and Florence Brown née Manship, was born on 23rd November 1891, at 49 Gresham Street, Belgrave, on her parent's first wedding anniversary.

Her first job was as a shoe machinist in Elmdale Street off the Loughborough Road, Belgrave. She later moved to work at T.G. Hunt on the Melton Road.

She married Oliver Hatfield and had three children, Gweneth Mabel, who died at the early age of six years of meningitis, Eva Dorothy, and John William.

In 1926, Oliver bought Kate a general grocer's shop at 82 Myrtle Road, Highfields, in Leicester, which she ran for 49 years. She retired on 31st December 1975.

Kate passed away on the 6th May 1977 aged 85, at Arbor House, Evington, Leicester, dying of 'old age'. Her funeral was at St Michael and All Angels, Belgrave.

Hatfield, Oliver John (1888 - 1952)

Oliver John was born at the Station House, Clifton Mill Station, Clifton upon Dunsmore, Rugby, in Warwickshire on 8th August 1888.

Oliver's family later moved to South Street, Rugby until his father, Robert Hatfield died in 1903. They then came to Leicester, where they lived at 66 Moira Street, Belgrave.

He worked at the British United Shoe Machinery Company as an engineer and when he married moved to 43 Wand Street, Belgrave. He later worked for Wildt, Mellor Bromley on Gipsy Lane.

He was married to Kate Brown at St Michael and All Angels Church on Melton Road, Belgrave and they had three children, Gweneth Mabel, Eva Dorothy and John William.

He died of pneumonia and diabetes aged 63 years, at Leicester Royal Infirmary, Marriott Ward, on 7th

February 1952, the day after King George VI passed away and his last words to his family were 'The King is dead'.

His funeral was held at St Michael and All Angels Church, Belgrave.

He now rests with Kate, his wife, who died in 1977 aged 85 years, Gweneth Mabel who died in 1921, aged six years and John William Hatfield, who died 1984 aged 63 years, his daughter and son.

It is interesting to note that Oliver John Hatfield's four times great grandmother, Mary Hatfield née Corrall from Husbands Bosworth was related by marriage, to Richard II and Edward, The Black Prince. She married David Hatfield who was a long-case clockmaker.

📖

Bamber, Mabel Elizabeth (1879 - 1945)

Mabel Elizabeth Hatfield was born on 27th December 1879 at the Station House, Clifton Mill Station, Clifton upon Dunsmore, Rugby in Warwickshire, daughter of Robert and Sarah Hatfield.

She married Harry Braithwaite Bamber, a telegraphist on 8th May 1909 in Wolverhampton and was widowed shortly afterwards in Ealing on 14th November 1914. Harry died of natural causes.

Harry and Mabel had two children, Dorothy and Frederick.

Mabel qualified as a State Registered Nurse, having been trained at the London Hospital. For a time she was a nurse at Uppingham School and was provided with a stone built cottage in School Lane, Uppingham.

Later she moved to Leicester and lived initially with her mother Sarah, at 66 Moira Street and then had her own house in Portman Street, moving to Rothley Street just before her final illness.

Mabel died of cancer on 8th February 1945, aged 65 years, at her daughter's home in Goscote Hall Road, Birstall, Leicester.

Hatfield, Sarah (1856 - 1922)

Sarah Dunkley was born on 17th August 1856 at Blisworth, Northampton.

On 27th June 1876 she married Robert Hatfield of Husbands Bosworth, who became station master at Clifton Mill Station, Clifton upon Dunsmore, Rugby, Warwickshire. The marriage having taken place at Blisworth, they lived initially at Mentmore Road, Linslade, Buckinghamshire, then the Station House, Clifton Mill and later in South Street Rugby.

They had nine children, three of whom died in infancy.

After Robert's death in 1903, Sarah moved to 66 Moira Street, Belgrave, Leicester.

Robert's siblings all lived in Leicester and one of her sons, Oliver, lodged with his aunt Elizabeth Allen in Harewood Street prior to Sarah moving to Leicester.

Sarah rented the house and Oliver, Kate and Gweneth lodged with her.

Sarah died on 27th March 1922, aged 66 years at 66 Moira Street. Her wish was to be buried near her granddaughter, Gweneth, who had died the year before. Hence the reason for the two family plots to be adjacent to each other.

Pemberton, Henry William (1923 - 1928)

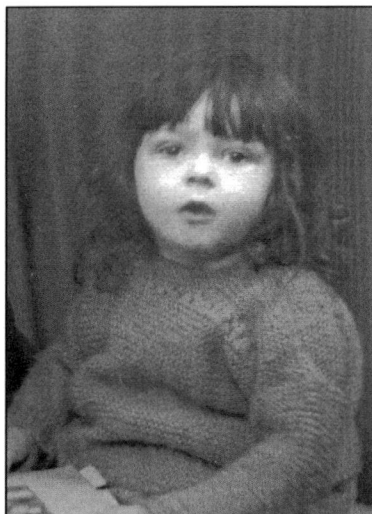

Henry William Pemberton was born in Leicester on 16th November 1923. He was the son of William Pemberton and Ada née Hatfield. Ada was the daughter of Robert and Sarah Hatfield.

Henry died on 27th May 1928 at 68 Moira Street, Belgrave of meningitis at the age of four years. How ironic it seems that he should die on the same date as his cousin Gweneth and of the same malady!

His parents were both buried at Gilroes Cemetery, in Leicester. He had one sibling, a sister Doris who lived to be 91 years of age (1920 – 2012) and she is buried with her parents.

Taylor, Ethel Maud (1886 - 1963)

Ethel Maud Hatfield was born on 21st December 1886 at the Station House, Clifton Mill Station, Clifton upon Dunsmore, Rugby, Warwickshire.

She moved to Leicester with the family following the death of her father Robert and lived at 66 Moira Street, Belgrave. She continued to live at this address throughout the rest of her life.

Ethel married Frederick Taylor at St Michael and All Angels Church, Melton Road, Belgrave on 1st September 1917.

They had two sons, Kenneth and Douglas.

Ethel worked with her sister Ada in the munitions factory in Belgrave Gate during the Great War and later became a housewife.

Ethel Maud died of pneumonia on 15th January 1963 at 66 Moira Street. She was 76 years old. She is laid to rest with her mother Sarah Hatfield who died in 1922

aged 66, her sister Mabel Elizabeth Bamber, who died in 1945, aged 65 years and her nephew Henry William Pemberton who died in 1928 aged four years. Ethel's husband Frederick died on 21st January 1979 aged 87 and his cremated remains were scattered at Gilroes.

Woollerton, Alice Ann (1866 - 1951)

Woollerton, John (1862 - 1928)

Alice Ann Tebbutt was born in 1866 in Leicester and married John Woollerton in 1883. The family moved to Leicester sometime in the 1900s.

Alice died in January 1951 aged 87 years, and was laid to rest on 30th January 1951.

John Woollerton was born in 1862 at Willoughby on the Wolds, the brother of Annie Eliza Darlaston. *(See Plot E776)*

He married Alice Ann Tebbutt in 1883 and sometime in the 1900s they moved to Leicester where he was a house painter, taking up residence at 111 Cooper Street, where John and Annie were to continue living until their deaths.

They had six children one of whom died, Ernest, aged six months in July 1903. At that time the address given in the cemetery records for Ernest was 2 Malt Office Lane.

John died in December 1928 aged 65 years. He is laid to rest with Alice Ann who died in January 1951 aged 87 years, his young son Ernest and another child from Alice's side of the family, Fred Tebbutt, who died in February 1905 aged five years.

Hubbard, Nellie Josephine (1913 - 2009)

Nellie Rodgers was born in 1913 youngest daughter to John and Harriet Rodgers. During her life, Nellie lived with her family at addresses in Belgrave and eventually in Shirley Street and Thurncourt Road.
She died in November 2009 at the great age of 96 years.

Rodgers, Harriet (1881 - 1940)

Harriet Brown was born to Thomas and Susan Brown in 1881. *(See Plot E221)*
She married John Rodgers and gave birth to William Reuben born 1906, John Albert born 1907, Enid Elizabeth born 1908, Eva A. born 1912 and Nellie Josephine born 1913.
During her marriage she and John lived in Mellor Street, off Checketts Road, a small cul-de-sac containing the local Junior school, The Conery, leading off Loughborough Road, and Mill Hill which is close by.
Harriet died in December 1940 aged 59 years.

Rodgers, John (1880 - 1955)

John Rodgers was born in 1880 and married Harriet Brown who was the daughter of Thomas and Susan Brown *(see Plot E221)* John and Harriet had a family of two boys and three girls.
John served in the Army Service Corps as a baker during the Boer War and later, on the 1911 Census, he is shown to be working for Russell and Co. Leicester as a Fitter for a brewers engineers. Later still John was to serve in the Great War.
During his life John lived at various addresses in Belgrave, and died in November 1955 aged 75 years. He was laid to rest in Belgrave Cemetery with Harriett who died in December 1940 aged 59 years and Nellie their daughter who died in November 2009 at the great age of 96 years.

John Rodgers mounted on his horse, whilst in military service

Beall, Maggie May (1909 - 2000)

Maggie May Perkins was born 13th August 1909 to Frederick and Ellen Perkins. Very little is known about her earlier life, but she worked at Corah's hosiery company where she met her future husband, Robert Edward Beall.

They were married on 25th July 1936 and had their only child, Roger on 24th June 1939.

She is remembered as a gentle, hard working mother who could make any type of clothes she wished to.

Her husband Robert had worked at Dunlop's during World War II making aeroplane tyres and also served in the Home Guard.

Maggie died on 7th February 2000 aged 90 years.

Perkins, Ellen (1882 - 1972)

Ellen Humber was born in 1882, the daughter of Frederick Humber and his wife Annie née Wilkinson.

Her father was listed as a Shoe Riveter and her mother was born in 1862.

Ellen also worked in the shoe making industry.

The date of her marriage to Frederick Perkins is unknown, but she had at least two children, Fred jnr. and Maggie May who was born in August 1909.

Ellen died in February 1972 aged 89.

Perkins, Frederick (1880 - 1946)

Frederick Perkins was born in 1880 and little is known about him until we find that he served on horseback in the Anglo-Boer War (1899-1902). There is a postcard still in the family, sent by him from Gibraltar on his way home from Africa, in possibly 1902, but the date is not fully visible.

At sometime he married Ellen Humber, unfortunately the date is unknown, as is the birth date of their son Fred but we do know that Maggie May, their daughter was born on 13th August 1909. There were no other children.

He was listed as a Wool Dyer's Labourer in 1909 and then a Motor Driver in 1936.

It is known that he was a Tram Driver in Leicester after the Second World War.

Frederick died in October 1946 and was living at 88 Harrison Road, Belgrave at that time. Ellen was laid to rest with him in February 1972 aged 89 years, and also Maggie May Beall, his daughter who died February 2000 aged 90 in the Manor Nursing Home, Lutterworth Road, Leicester. It is not clear where Fred his son is laid to rest.

Postcard received by family from Frederick on his way home from Africa

Darlaston, Annie Eliza (1865 -1928)

Annie Eliza Woollerton was born in Willoughby on the Wolds, on 21st March 1865. She was baptised on 1st August 1865 at Willoughby. Her brother was John Woollerton *(see Plot E731)*.

On 22nd October 1882 she married Thomas William Darlaston at the parish church, Belgrave and they were to have five children, including Lydia.

It is not known if Annie had employment during her married life, but she and Thomas lived in several addresses in Belgrave during their marriage.

She died in April 1928, aged 64 years at 74 Roberts Road, Belgrave and was laid to rest on 18th April 1928.

Darlaston, Thomas William (1864 - 1942)

Thomas was born in Bedworth on 21st April 1864 Warwickshire and was baptised on 3rd September 1868 at All Saints Church, Bedworth.

He worked in the hosiery trade

Thomas married Annie Eliza Woollerton on 22nd October 1882 at the parish church in Belgrave.

Thomas and Annie had five children, one of them a daughter, Lydia.

From 1891 he lived with his family at various addresses in Belgrave.

He died aged 77 years on 25th February 1942 at 3 Limber Crescent, Braunstone Estate, Leicester, his death certificate stating he was a retired hosiery winder and his cause of death was coal gas poisoning, suicide whilst the balance of his mind was disturbed. An inquest was held on 27th February 1942 and he was buried on 2nd March 1942.

Moore, Alma Kathleen (1923 - 1929)

Alma was the daughter of Lydia and Sidney Moore, born in 1923 at 6 Dundonald Road, Belgrave and was baptised on 15th April 1923.

Her parents knew she would not live long as she had heart and other medical problems.

The night before Alma died, while she had a bath, she sang "I'm forever blowing bubbles".

Her mother Lydia went upstairs the next morning and found she had died in bed.

Alma Kathleen was buried on 5th March 1929.

Moore, Dennis (1926 - 1931)

Dennis was born in 1926 at Dundonald Road, Belgrave, the son of Lydia and Sidney Moore and grandson of Thomas and Annie Darlaston, and was baptised on 3rd February 1926.

He drowned in the canal at the bottom of Dundonald Road. He was playing with Mary Sharp and George Sharp when he tumbled into the water. The Sharp children told their mother and she told Lydia. Although Lydia along with her eldest son Leslie went to help they were too late. It had been very cold with snow.

Dennis was buried on 12th March 1931.

His father Sidney Moore, died on 16th March 1956 and was cremated after a funeral at St. Mark's Church, Belgrave. Lydia his mother, died on 3rd January 1965 and was cremated after her funeral on 7th January at St Mark's too.

Moore, Iris Nellie (1921 - 1921)

Iris was born early in 1921 at 6 Dundonald Road, Belgrave, daughter of Lydia and Sidney Moore and granddaughter of Thomas William and Annie Eliza Darlaston.

Iris was baptised at St Mark's Church, Belgrave, on 21st March 1921 but died soon after of meningitis, aged five months approximately. She was buried at Belgrave Cemetery on 15th August 1921.

Iris Nellie is laid to rest with her grandmother Annie Eliza and grandfather Thomas William Darlaston, her sister Alma Kathleen aged five years, 1929 and her brother Dennis, aged five years 1931. Her brother Leslie, who died in 1942, is buried elsewhere in Belgrave Cemetery. *(See Plot C704)*

Southwell, Arthur (1872 - 1926)

Arthur & Ada Southwell with first-born son Arthur *(standing)* and Leonard on Ada's lap

Arthur Southwell was originally from Wolverhampton where he was born in 1872.

Little is known about his early life, but he married Ada Smart who had been born at 45 Willow Bridge Street, Leicester on 12th May 1871.

Their marriage took place on 4th June 1892 at the Parish Church of Belgrave St. Peters and at that time Arthur was living at 33 Holden Street and Ada at 34 Shirley Street, Belgrave.

After their marriage, Arthur and Ada Southwell lived at 9 Shirley Street, and Arthur was employed as a finisher in the boot and shoe trade.

They must have had a very distressing time as parents.

Their first sad loss was their second son, Lance Corporal Leonard George Southwell who died in the battle of Loos in the Great War on 13th October 1915 aged 19.

Seven years later on 8th April 1922 they lost another son, Ernest, aged 16 to tuberculosis, and a month later on 14th May 1922 a second son, Henry aged 21 also succumbed to the disease.

Sadness continued on 6th December 1924 as another daughter, Doris aged 22 also died of tuberculosis, then two years later Arthur died on 24th April 1926 aged 54 years of the same disease. He was laid to rest in Belgrave Cemetery with his two sons Ernest and Henry and his daughter Doris.

So in the space of seven years Ada had lost four of her eight children and also her husband and we can only imagine how hard it must have been nursing them all, with very little money coming in and the expense of funerals etc. money must have been hard to find.

Unfortunately, the sadness did not end there, as on 12th June 1932, Ada lost yet another child, her married daughter, Edith Evelyn Wilkinson, aged 34, to this dreadful disease. *(See Plot C628)*

Leonard Southwell killed in action WWI

Despite all this unhappiness Ada Southwell, widow of Arthur, was a super person to all who knew her and was a joy to be with. Despite the hard life she had, she lived to the ripe old age of 93.

Ada died on 13th June 1964 at De Montfort Nursing Home, Narborough Road, Leicester and was cremated at Gilroes Cemetery where her ashes were scattered in the Garden of Remembrance.

It is not known by the present family why she was not placed in Belgrave Cemetery, but as there are no markers or headstones on the graves, placement of the ashes would have been difficult, so perhaps this was the reason.

Harris, Arthur Craddock (1872 - 1940)

Arthur Craddock Harris was born on 15th November 1872 in Leicester.
He is mentioned in the 1881 Census aged eight, living with his parents, Thomas Harris, aged 53, employed as a Railway Engine Driver, having been born in Narborough, Leicestershire. His mother, Ann Harris, was born in Leicester sometime around 1830.

At this time Arthur has three siblings, Emma, Fanny and Victor all living at 55 Upper Charnwood Street.

By the 1891 Census, Arthur has left school and is working as an Engine Cleaner, and his mother is now head of the household at 101 Charnwood Street. Arthur now shares his home with two of his mother's grand daughters, Alice and Polly Austin, both still at school.

On the 1901 Census, Arthur is not mentioned, as later in 1891 as a 19 year old he enlisted in the Royal Artillery and subsequently fought in the Boer War being presented with the King's Medal for fighting in the South African Campaign at De Klipdrift on 7th March 1902. This could have been where he received an injury to his foot.

He married Florence Copson on 13th April 1903 and on the 1911 Census his family is living at 69 Marfitt Street, Belgrave, Arthur working as a Hosiery Warehouseman and the couple have a daughter, Beatrice who was born in 1904 in Leicester.

Having remained in the Reserves and receiving further training, at the age of 42 in 1914, he was called up for active service in the Great War. During this period of time he was promoted to Warrant Officer and served in both Belgium and France and it was from there that his daughter aged 12, received a Christmas card, which the family still have in their possession. The card will be a hundred years old in 2016.

It reads:

"To Beatty, From Dada 1916, To my Dear daughter

Beatrice with love and best wishes for a Happy Xmas and a brighter New Year, From Dada x".

Arthur was subsequently honourably discharged on 10th August 1918. He was to see the beginning of yet another war before he died on 15th August 1940, aged 67 years. On the kerbstone around his grave were the words, "His duty nobly done".

Some of this information came to the family in a surprising way.

In 2003, a cousin of the contributor received a phone call from people living in their grandparents former house and were told they had found property in the attic, which appertained to their family. When they visited they were astounded to be presented with a glass framed certificate, with their grandfather's name on it stating he had been disabled and 'Honourably Discharged' from the Great War on 10th August 1918.

Harris, Florence (1876 - 1955)

Florence Copson was born on 25th August 1876, in Leicester.

On the 1881 Census she is four years old and shown as living at 49 Twycross Street, Leicester with her parents John Copson, aged 29 and a gas fitter born in Rowell, Essex. Her mother, Betsy A. Copson aged 29 born in 1852 at Corby Northamptonshire is employed as a Machinist.

Florence has one older brother at this time, Walter J Copson aged six.

By the 1891 Census, Florence aged 15, is a General Servant Domestic living at Wood Street, Hinckley. She is employed, along with a housekeeper, to James Toom, a Hosiery Manufacturer of Earl Shilton origins. In the possession of the family is a note book which Florence used for recipes whilst working at Swinford Lodge.

By 1901 Florence has returned home to her father's house, at 101 Charnwood Street, (it would appear that her father had married Ellen Stanage née Harris in 1889, Betsy having died towards the end on 1887) and Florence is making her living as a Tailoress. Perhaps Florence had training from own her mother at some point. Florence now also has a sister, Edith E. Copson, aged 10 years.

In the late spring of 1903, Florence married Arthur Craddock Harris.

Beatrice Harris had been born in 1904 and Florence wasn't employed at this time. She went on to have another child named John who later became a Battery Quarter Master Sergeant in the 153rd Leicestershire Yeomanry Field Regiment. Florence was a very accomplished tailoress for one of the main gents outfitters in Leicester, and also an excellent cook.

Florence died on 16th December 1955, aged 79 years. Arthur had passed away on 15th August 1940 aged 68 years. At the time of their deaths they were living at 10 Gleneagles Avenue, Belgrave.

Ireland, Allan Reginald (1923 - 2004)

Born on 26th August 1923, Allan Reginald was the only son of Walter and Mabel Ireland. He joined up when he was 17 or 18 and became a gunner in the 22nd Dragoon Tank Regiment and took part in the D-Day landings in Normandy and after the war suffered many years of shell-shock.

During a holiday in Belgium in 1953, which he was taking alone, he had a chance meeting with Elisabeth Van Hoof at the hotel in Brussels where she worked. It led to marriage on 29th April 1954 at the Leicester Register Office, and 45 happy years together.

Two children soon completed the family.

Allan and Elisabeth's first house was on Dean Road, off Catherine Street, Leicester and then in 1956 they moved into Allan's parents' house, 14 Wavertree Drive, Belgrave as Walter and Mabel had moved further up the road into number 68.

Allan was a butcher and owned a shop on Victoria Road East, Leicester, retiring at the age of 62. He passed away on 3rd August 2004 aged 80 years.

Ireland, Elisabeth (1918 - 1999)

Elisabeth Konz was one of eight children of Jean and Ann Konz and was born in Mersch, Luxembourg, on 11th August 1918.

Having lost her mother when she was in her early teens, Elisabeth left school at a young age to help her father manage the home and family.

Her father owned a small quarry and following an unfortunate accident with explosives he had lost a hand and had been fitted to wear a hook.

Elisabeth married Armand Van Hoof in 1940 and they lived in the town of Leuven in Belgium. She was widowed in 1944 aged 26 and she left Leuven to find work and start a new life in Brussels.

After an unlikely meeting there during 1953 she met Allan Ireland. On 29th April 1954, they were married at Leicester Register Office, with an interpreter present to help her as her English wasn't yet perfect.

Odette Katherine was born in 1955 followed by Frederick Reginald in 1958.

Elisabeth passed away on 9th March 1999 aged 81 years and was laid to rest at Belgrave Cemetery and was joined by Allan on 3rd August 2004, aged 80 years. Also in the grave are Susan Isabella Ireland who died 30th September 1932, aged 71 years and also Henry Ireland who died in May 1948 aged 86 years. They were the grand-parents of Allan Reginald Ireland.

CONCLUSION

This research has encouraged some of our contributors to continue researching their family trees and tell their younger family members about their past lives. I hope our book will encourage more of this, as we know how frustrating it is to realise that we didn't talk to our grandparents enough before they died.

It has also highlighted how delicate photographs from the 19th and 20th century become, particularly if not kept in good conditions.

Some of the photographs which you see here received many hours of repair work due to scratches, tears, holes, fading and deterioration. I hope you agree that their loss would have been tragic. Some could not be included as identification was uncertain.

Please cherish these gems from the past, after all 'a picture paints a thousand words'.

If you have read this book and you have family members who are at rest in Belgrave Cemetery but are not included, please contact Friends of Belgrave Cemetery to insert an entry in the next edition. We would love to hear from you.

If you are not already a member of the 'Friends' why not join us? We issue a newsletter each quarter year and your commitment time is as much or little as you wish.

Please see our website on www.friendsofbelgravecemetery.org.uk where contact details can be found along with a history of the cemetery and forthcoming events.

MEMORIES OF BELGRAVE CEMETERY

You entered at the Red Hill end through the iron gates; the drive was lined with chestnut trees each side leading to a house, lived in by Mr Ward. He took care of the cemetery. On the left hand side there is a monument for him. Turning right by the house there was a large greenhouse with live grape vines – one green, one black, an old tap for water, a basket for rubbish and a seat.

Walk straight on, take the path on the left and you came to a very large building. One was a chapel, the other a church. Also toilets, a seat and a tap. Taking the path to the right you came to the allotments and the railway station. To the bottom of that path was St Margaret's playing fields. You would pass a very old pump for water then straight on and back to Mr Ward's house.

Children were not allowed without adults, and you had to be quiet. Also I have a feeling the graves were not flat like they are today. We went regularly until the war then things changed. I came back home in 1979 and continued visiting. I remember seeing the horses bringing the hearse to the church or chapel. I don't go as often as I would like.

Peggy Marston
1915 - 2010
Late member of Friends of Belgrave Cemetery

She Loved This Place

INDEX OF ENTRIES – SURNAME ORDER

B

F

Fantham, Cissy May (1903 – 1995)	D848	84
Foulds, Arthur (1870 - 1944)	B302	27
Foulds, Mary (1868 - 1935)	B302	27

G

Garner, Anne (1850 – 1954)	C212	41
Glover, William George (1907 – 1949)	C383	53
Godsall, Gladys Beatrice (1904 – 1993)	D1079	97
Godsall, May Louisa (1878 – 1939)	D1079	98
Godsall, William (1877 – 1955)	D1079	99
Green, William (1835 – 1900)	D918	88
Guilford, Charles Thomas (1880 - 1966)	D349	76
Guilford, Florence Ann (1873 – 1955)	D349	76
Guilford, George (1827 - 1891)	A288	20
Guilford, Harriett (1830? - 1907)	A288	20
Guilford, Jane (1858 - 1929)	D349	77
Guilford, John Thomas (1857 – 1932)	D349	77

H

Harris, Arthur Craddock (1872 – 1940)	E919	122
Harris, Florence (1876 – 1955)	E919	124
Hatfield, Gweneth Mabel (1914 - 1921)	E710	108
Hatfield, John William (1921 - 1984)	E710	108
Hatfield, Kate (1891 - 1977)	E710	109
Hatfield, Oliver John (1888 – 1952)	E710	109
Hatfield, Sarah (1856 - 1922)	E711	111
Holliland, Bertha (1873 - 1940)	C548	56
Holliland, Bertram (1897 - 1928)	C832	61
Holliland, George Clipson (1872 - 1943)	C548	56
Horner, William Rudkin (1883 - 1912)	B518	30
Hoskins, Thomas (1878 – 1952)	B745	32
Hubbard, Nellie Josephine (1913 – 2009)	E763	114
Hughes, Ann (1864 - 1940)	B33	25
Hughes, John Augustus (1865 - 1937)	B33	25

I

Ireland, Allan Reginald (1923 - 2004)	E958	125
Ireland, Elisabeth (1918 – 1999)	E958	125

J

Jackson, Annie Elizabeth (1863 - 1932)	D299	73
Jackson, Gertrude (1898 – 1965)	D299	73
Jackson, Walter (1863 - 1935)	D299	74

K

Keable, Ernest (1886 - 1969)	E375	106
Keable, Ethel (1885 - 1949)	E375	106
Keeling, Percival Turney (1881 - 1941)	C373	50
King, Hazel (1934 – 2009)	B302	27
Kingston, Tom (1888? - 1943)	E256	105
Kirk, Leonard Hairsine (1888 - 1921)	A29	3

L

Larratt, Edward (1874 - 1945)	C383	54
Larratt, Susan Maria (1872 – 1942)	C383	54

M

Manship, Arthur (1883 – 1919)	A185	11
Mason, Arthur (1878 - 1925)	C924	64
Mason, Clement Samuel (1903 – 1950)	C924	65
Mason, Edith Laura (1875 – 1931)	C924	65
Mason, John Henry (1871 - 1938)	C887	62
Mawby, Elizabeth Annie (1848 – 1920)	A159	8
Middleton, Ann (1873 - 1938)	D1011	90
Middleton, Arthur Thomas (1873 - 1957)	D1011	90
Moore, Alma Kathleen (1923 - 1929)	E776	118
Moore, Clara (1869 - 1955)	D298	72
Moore, Dennis (1926 – 1931)	E776	119
Moore, Iris Nellie (1921 – 1921)	E776	119
Moore, Leslie (1912 - 1942)	C704	60
Moore, Lily (1883 – 1971)	D298	72
Moore, Nodous (1847 - 1920)	D484	78
Moore, Susannah (1846 - 1925)	D484	79
Moore, Thomas (1879 - 1911)	D484	79
Moore, Walter (1889 - 1915)	D484	79

P

Peel, Mary Ellen (1861 - 1960)	A390	21
Pemberton, Henry William (1923 - 1928)	E711	112

Penn, Jabez (1843 – 1920)	B746	34
Perkins, Ellen (1882 – 1972)	E764	116
Perkins, Frederick (1880 - 1946)	E764	117
Powell, John Barnett (1854 – 1923)	C309	45
Pretty, Emma (1858 – 1904)	A159	9
Pugh, Henry (1915 - 2000)	C46	38
Pugh, Maud (1910 - 2001)	C46	40

R

Radford, Grace Alexandria (1900 - 1998)	D848	85
Robinson, Elizabeth May (1908 - 1995)	D1026	93
Robinson, Harry Edwin (1902 - 1975)	D1026	94
Rodgers, Harriet (1881 - 1940)	E763	114
Rodgers, John (1880 – 1955)	E763	114
Roper, Samuel Henry (1848? – 1890)	A160	10
Ross, Joseph (1838 - 1906)	D813	83

S

Savage, Esther (1866 - 1923)	D1183	100
Savage, William (1866 - 1924)	D1183	100
Smith, Hannah (1884 - 1965)	D238	68
Smith, Jane (1912 - 1960)	D238	68
Smith, Noah (1879 - 1960)	D238	69
Southwell, Arthur (1872 - 1926)	E892	120
Squires, Lizzie (1861? - 1936)	C313	46
Squires, William George (1856 - 1944)	C313	47
Sumner, William (1894 - 1943)	B302	28

T

Taylor, Ethel Maud (1886 - 1963)	E711	112
Thompson, Charles (1863 - 1925)	C346	48
Thompson, John Ernest (1887 - 1891)	A286	18
Thompson, Mary Ann (1864 – 1935)	C346	49
Toach, Gladys (1908 – 1988)	D115	67
Tomlinson, Norah (1896 - 1959)	C277	44
Tomlinson, Walter Hamlet (1893 - 1942)	C277	44

V

Vann, Harry William (1864 – 1915)	A249	17
Vann, Sarah Ann (1862 - 1950)	A249	17

W

INDEX OF ENTRIES – SECTION / PLOT ORDER

	SECTION B	
Section/Plot	**Name**	**Page**